PLAYING FOR KEEPS IN STOCKS & FUTURES

Wiley Trading

PLAYING FOR KEEPS IN STOCKS & FUTURES

Three Top Trading Strategies That Consistently Beat the Markets

Tom Bierovic

John Wiley & Sons

Published by John Wiley & Sons, Inc., New York
Published simultaneously in Canada.

Library of Congress Cataloging-in-Publication Data

Bierovic, Thomas A.
    Playing for keeps in stocks and futures : three top trading strategies
that consistently beat the markets / by Tom Bierovic.
        p. cm.—(Wiley trading)
    Includes index.
    ISBN 0-471-14547-5 (cloth : alk. paper)
    1. Stocks. 2. Futures. 3. Speculation. I. Title. II. Series.

    HG4661 .B54 2001
    332.63'22—dc21   2001046611

Printed in the United States of America.

10 9 8 7 6 5 4 3 2 1

This book is dedicated
with respect, gratitude and love
to my parents, Frank and Mary Bierovic
and to my wife, Laurie Bierovic.

CONTENTS

ACKNOWLEDGMENTS

Many wise and generous people helped me on my journey to become a trader and to write this book, so I'm pleased to have this opportunity to thank them.

My dad got me started in the trading business when I was just 12 years old, and he and my mom have stood by me through the myriad ups and downs of a trader's life.

Tim Slater, the creator of CompuTrac—the world's first technical analysis software—and the director of the renowned Technical Analysis Group (TAG) trading conferences, invited me to present my first trading workshop at TAG 13 in 1991. Forty countries and more than a lifetime's worth of adventures and misadventures later, I wish we could start over and do it all again.

Nelson Freeburg, Chuck LeBeau, John Murphy, Steve Nison, and Jack Schwager all taught me market truths that I never would have figured out if left to my own devices.

While we were traveling internationally, presenting seminars for Dow Jones/Telerate, Linda Raschke taught me five of her favorite moving average convergence-divergence patterns (MACDs). Because the MACD setups in *Playing for Keeps* are my variations on three of those patterns, Linda deserves a special thanks for her contribution to this book.

Pamela van Giessen, Gail Farrar, and Steve Sullivan made many suggestions that improved the book's accuracy, clarity, and focus; Jennifer MacDonald and Alexia Meyers ably guided the manuscript through the production labyrinth.

My wife Laurie helped so much with this project that I wanted to include her name with mine on the book as coauthor; however, with characteristic modesty, she declined. This book could not have been produced without Laurie's assistance.

My deepest and most sincere thanks to all of you.

T.A.B.

PREFACE

The objective of *Playing for Keeps in Stocks and Futures* is to provide traders (and aspiring traders) with three winning strategies—*First Prize*, *R2D2*, and *Triple Play*—that they can employ successfully in today's financial markets. The strategies can be used to trade both stocks and futures in all time frames from one minute (if you're so inclined) to the daily, weekly, or even monthly time frames. I trade stocks and futures with these three strategies every day, focusing mainly on the daily time frame.

This book is written for people who already have a basic knowledge of the financial markets and the procedure for making trades; therefore, it doesn't include basic information such as what a stock is, selecting a broker, or placing an order. The reading list near the end of this book includes my recommendations for books that provide that type of background information. I also haven't included information on computers and software that you can use to trade because that information is readily available elsewhere.

Playing for Keeps in Stocks and Futures begins with three brief chapters: The first offers several reasons why trading is such a desirable endeavor, the second reveals the most important fact about a market's price swings, and the third introduces the three components of a complete trading strategy.

The fourth chapter, *First Prize*, begins by explaining all the technical tools used in this book's three strategies and goes on to present my *First Prize* strategy. Chapters five and six cover the *R2D2* and *Triple Play* strategies. Chapter seven offers several suggestions about the psychology of trading, and the appendices present my recommended reading lists and the answers to chapter quizzes.

I hope that *Playing for Keeps in Stocks and Futures* will help you to achieve your trading goals. Make sure your goals are high enough, because the sky's the limit for a successful trader!

Tom Bierovic
Palm Beach Gardens, Florida
July 2001

PLAYING FOR KEEPS IN STOCKS & FUTURES

INTRODUCTION

One of the best things that can happen to a person is to get an early start on learning something that he enjoys and has an aptitude for—especially if the thing is so hard to do that the rewards are substantial for those who can master it. Tiger Woods is a perfect example: Tiger started learning to play golf when he was just old enough to stand up and maintain his balance while swinging a tiny golf club. He enjoyed golf even as a child, and he had a remarkable talent for it. The rest is history.

Of course, I'm definitely *not* the Tiger Woods of trading (I don't know if *any*one is the Tiger Woods of *any*thing else), but I did get an early start on something I enjoyed and had at least a little bit of aptitude for: trading stocks and futures. My dad had a seat on the old Chicago Open Board of Trade, and when I was just 12 years old, I began to earn my allowance by getting commodity prices from the daily newspaper and maintaining my dad's charts and technical indicators for him. During summer vacations, I worked on the floor of the exchange, keeping intraday charts on corn, wheat, and soybeans while my dad traded in the pits. I made the first trade for my own account in 1970, on my twenty-first birthday, and I have been enjoying the daily battle in the market arena ever since. *Playing for Keeps in Stocks and Futures* is my attempt to make a contribution to the industry that's been so generous to my family and me over the years.

I hope you will enjoy and profit from *First Prize, R2D2,* and *Triple Play,* the three strategies presented in this book. If you learn the strategies thoroughly, apply them resolutely, and manage your trades wisely, you'll be playing for keeps in stocks and futures before you can say, "Tiger made *how* much money last year?"

T.A.B.

Chapter 1

WHY TRADE?

Few human activities have been so exhaustively studied during the past fifty years [this was written in 1948] from so many angles and by so many different sorts of people, as has the buying and selling of corporate securities. The rewards which the stock market holds out to those who read it right are enormous; the penalties it extracts from careless, dozing, or "unlucky" investors are calamitous—no wonder it has attracted some of the world's most astute accountants, analysts, and researchers, along with a motley crew of eccentrics, mystics, and "hunch players" and a multitude of just ordinary hopeful citizens

—Robert D. Edwards and John Magee, *Technical Analysis of Stock Trends* (John Magee Inc., Springfield, Massachusetts, 1948)

Trading the financial markets may well be the best business opportunity in the world for the twenty-first–century entrepreneur. Following are 10 of the reasons why trading is such a compelling pursuit.

1. You can live anywhere in the world and trade from the comfort and convenience of your home.

2. Trading has a low start-up cost and low overhead. You can open your trading account with as little as $2,500 to $5,000 and limit your expenses to the cost of discounted commissions, a computer, and an Internet service provider.

3. You can set your own daily schedule. Many traders simply check their positions in the evening to see how their trades performed that day, look for a few new trading opportunities for the next day, and make any adjustments they consider necessary. You do not have to follow the markets during the trading day if you don't want to or if it's not convenient for you.

4. You can take vacations whenever you choose by simply closing your positions and starting fresh when you return home.

5. As an independent trader, you have no expensive retail space or suite of offices, no inventory, no customers, no employees, no lawsuits, and no bureaucratic interference: It's just you and the markets you trade.

6. No advanced education, licensing, or certification is required if you trade only for your own account. All the information you need about the markets and trading is readily and affordably available in books, seminars, audio-video courses, and on the Internet.

7. Your financial results are based solely on your own skill and effort, and you can enjoy a potentially un-limited income for the rest of your life.

8. Only about 10% of traders win consistently. That's great news because you can make it into that group of winners who divide up all the money that is lost by the other 90% of traders. A game in which 50% of traders win and divide up what the other 50% lose would not be nearly as rewarding.

9. Active traders can enjoy a favorable tax situation by declaring *trader status* on their tax returns. (Make sure you understand the relevant laws com-pletely or get professional tax advice before you file as an active trader.)

10. You can even pass your best trading strategies down to your children and grandchildren and make trad-ing a family business for generations to come. That's one of the legacies my parents have passed on to me, and I know other families who have also built trading "dynasties" with great success.

In the next chapter, you'll begin learning how to take advantage of the tremendous opportunities that trading offers.

Chapter 1 Quiz

1. The high startup costs and exorbitant overhead make trading a suitable activity only for people who are already rich.

True   False

2. One of the disadvantages of trading is that traders have to spend all day in front of their monitors watching the markets.

True   False

3. If a trader trades only for his or her own account, he or she faces very little governmental interference or bureaucratic red tape.

True   False

4. Studies show that in the long run about 50% of traders are winners, and about 50% of traders are losers.

True   False

Chapter 2

PRICE SWINGS 101

Sound judgment, good intuition, foresight and wisdom do not come about overnight by reading a book or adopting a method or discovering a formula. These invaluable assets on which our vital predictive processes in life are based constitute a whole lifelong process of self-education. It is not easy, but it is the only way
—John Magee, *Analyzing Bar Charts for Profit*
(John Magee Inc., Boston, 1994)

The most obvious and most important characteristic of price movement in the financial markets is the extreme and continuous variation in the duration and magnitude of price swings (see Figures 2.1 and 2.2). *Duration* is the number of periods (minutes, hours, days, etc.) that a price swing lasts, and *magnitude* is the number of points up or down that a price swing extends. To make it easy to identify price swings, I'll construct a channel based on moving averages of highs and lows and overlay the channel on some price charts later in this discussion. (Moving averages smooth price data to make the underlying trend

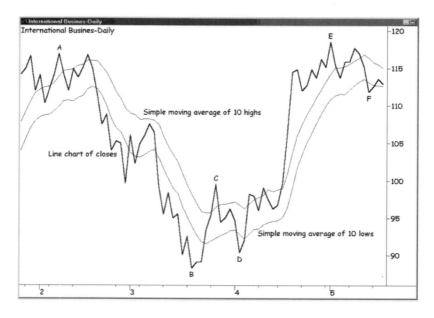

Figure 2.1 Price swings A–B and D–E are big in both duration and magnitude, whereas price swings B–C and C–D are small. We can't tell yet if price swing E–F is going to be a big swing or a small one.

easier to identify. To calculate a simple moving average of 10 closes, for example, add the last 10 closes and divide the total by 10. As the average is calculated and plotted for each new period under consideration [e.g. every five minutes, every day, or every week] the average moves across the page or computer screen, hence the term *moving average*.)

I define price swings as follows: a bullish (upward) price swing begins at the lowest close below the moving-average channel and ends at the highest close above the channel; a bearish (downward) price swing begins at the

12

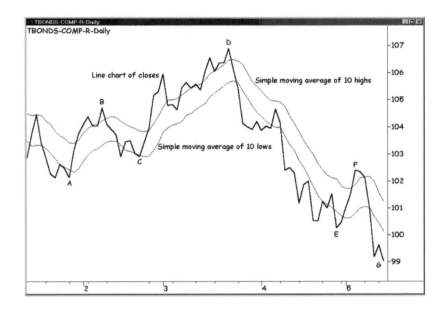

Figure 2.2 Price swings A–B, B–C, and E–F are small in duration and magnitude, whereas price swings C–D and D–E are big. We don't know yet if price swing F–G will be a big swing or a small one.

highest close above the moving-average channel and ends at the lowest close below the channel.

The extreme and continuous variation of price swings makes it possible for financial markets to exist and for traders to have an opportunity to speculate profitably. If markets fluctuated smoothly, consistently, and repetitiously in strong trends or well-defined trading ranges, even traders with mediocre skills could correctly anticipate the duration and magnitude of every price swing. If price fluctuations were easy to predict, there would be no difference of opinion among traders. If everyone knew how many time periods a price swing would continue in its current direction and how many points higher or lower prices would be at the end of the price swing, who would take the opposite side of the trades we wish to initiate? Therefore, a difference of opinion about the potential duration and magnitude of price swings is necessary for traders to have the opportunity to buy and sell. This difference of opinion is strongest at what I call *critical points* within every trend, when traders have to decide if a countertrend price move is a short-term reaction within the existing trend or the beginning of a trend reversal. (see Figures 2.3 and 2.4) In this discussion, I'll

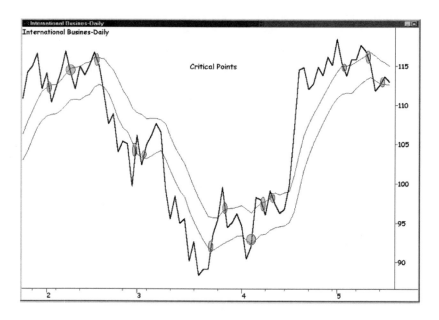

Figure 2.3 This figure highlights 13 critical points in a chart of IBM. Note that the main trend resumed after some of the critical points but reversed after other critical points.

14

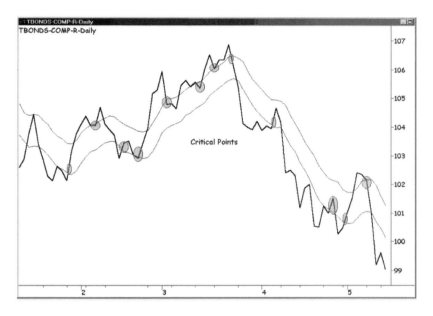

Figure 2.4   This figure highlights 12 critical points in bond futures. After some critical points, the main trend resumed, but after others, the main trend reversed.

define a critical point in an uptrend as a countertrend price decline into the moving-average channel and a critical point in a downtrend as a countertrend price rally into the channel.

Of course, other traders have different ways of identifying trends and countertrends; we don't all use a moving-average channel. However, the principle remains the same: When prices begin to fall within an uptrend, traders have to decide if the decline is part of the normal give-and-take within the uptrend or if the decline is more likely to continue and become a new downtrend. Conversely, when prices begin to rise within a downtrend, traders have to decide if the rally is part of the down-trend's typical zigzag, or if the rally is more likely to continue and commence a new uptrend.

When a market has begun to decline within an up-trend, some traders buy, believing that the uptrend will reassert itself, whereas others sell, believing that the decline is the beginning of a new downtrend. Conversely, when a market has begun to rally within a downtrend, some traders sell short, believing that the downtrend will resume in the near future, while others buy, believing that the rally is the beginning of a new uptrend. Sometimes the traders who bet on a resumption of the underlying trend are correct, and sometimes the traders who bet on a reversal of the underlying trend are correct.

The good news is that we will never have to worry about freely traded financial markets becoming too consistent, too predictable, or too comprehensible—they never have been and never will be. The extreme and continuous variation in the duration and magnitude of price swings will continue to create differences of opinion so that at any given moment some traders are anxious to buy while others are eager to sell. The trick, of course, is to make the correct decision at critical points more often than most other traders do—and that's really what *Playing for Keeps in Stocks and Futures* is all about.

Chapter 2 Quiz

1. Stock prices usually fluctuate in price swings that are approximately equal in duration and magnitude.

    True   False

2. In *Playing for Keeps,* critical points occur in countertrend price declines during uptrends and countertrend price rallies during downtrends.

    True   False

3. A trader who identifies a critical point in an uptrend should buy; one who identifies a critical point in a downtrend should sell short.

    True   False

4. The extreme and continuous variation in the duration and magnitude of price swings creates opportunities for traders to buy and sell.

    True   False

Chapter 3

THE THREE COMPONENTS OF A TRADING STRATEGY

*To many people, the stock market is a confusing and con-
fused melee in which prices move helter-skelter without
rhyme or reason. But this confusion is, to some extent, a
confusion in their own minds, since they do not understand
the complicated forces and the detail of procedure that actually cause stock prices to advance or decline. They might feel
the same sense of meaningless movement that a visitor to a
textile mill might feel the first time he saw the operation of
an automatic loom. He might not understand at first sight
that the strange shifts of the jacquard mechanism were not
meaningless, but were directed toward the orderly creation
of a definite pattern in the cloth which would have meaning
to anyone when he saw the finished product.*
—John Magee, *Analyzing Bar Charts for Profit*
(John Magee Inc., Boston, 1994)

Successful traders know that a winning strategy requires
more than a vague notion of buying a stock or commodity and hoping it goes up. A winning strategy consists of
three components: *setups*, *entries*, and *exits*.

Setups alert you that a trading opportunity has developed. Setups don't actually get you *into* a trade; instead, they tell you that market conditions have become *favorable* for a trade. Three consecutive higher closes is one example of a buy setup; a symmetrical triangle pattern is another one. Examples of setups to sell short are a five-day average of closes crossing below a 15-day average of closes, or a close below the lowest low of the last five days.

After a setup, entry conditions that you specify must be met before a trade can be initiated. Entries actually get you into a trade. An example of a long entry is buying today one tick above yesterday's high; another example is buying today when prices cross above a three-day average of highs. Examples of short entries are selling short when prices penetrate the lower line of a symmetrical triangle pattern, or selling short when prices drop by more than one average daily range from yesterday's close.

Exits, of course, get you out of a trade. Initial protective stops, trailing stops, and profit targets are three types of exits.

Initial protective stops are designed to limit your original risk on a trade. An example of an initial protective stop for a long position is an order to sell if the price falls below last week's low; an example for a short position is an order to cover your shorts if the price rises more than $2.00 per share above your entry price.

Trailing stops are set below the current price for a long position and above the current price for a short position. When a market is moving your way, you adjust the trailing stop to lock in an increasing amount of your open profits. For example, if you're in a long position and the market's trending higher, you can keep raising your trailing stop to just below the lowest low of the last three days; if you're in a short position and the market's falling, you can lower your trailing stop to just above the three-day high.

Profit targets are another way to exit a trade. *Profit targets*, which close out a trade when the price reaches your specified objective, are set above the current price if you're long and below the current price if you're short—the opposite of trailing stops. An example of a profit-target exit for a long position is to sell when your open profit in the trade is equal to three times your initial risk on the trade; an example for a short position is to close out the trade when prices hit last year's low.

Understanding the three components of a trading strategy—setups, entries, and exits—already puts you a big step ahead of many other traders. Your next task is to learn the *specific* setups, entries, and exits in my *First Prize*, *R2D2*, and *Triple Play* strategies.

Chapter 3 Quiz

1. The key to successful trading is knowing when to buy.

    True   False

2. Setups tell traders that market conditions may be favorable for a trade.

    True   False

3. A trader who identifies a setup should enter a new trade as soon as possible.

    True   False

4. An initial protective stop is designed to limit a trader's risk on a trade.

    True   False

5. A trailing stop is set above a stock's current price in a long position and below the current price in a short position.

    True   False

6. An effective trailing stop should lock in some open profits while giving a stock some room to run.

    True   False

7. A profit-target exit closes out a trade when a specified price objective is reached.

    True   False

Chapter 4

FIRST PRIZE

The market will continue to go up and down in the future as it has in the past. Your technical knowledge will save you from "buying at the top" in the final climactic blow-off, and it will save you from selling everything in a fit of depression and disgust when the bottom is being established. In your studies of past market action you have a strong shield and buckler against the sudden thrusts that surprise and often defeat the novice trader.
            —Robert D. Edwards and John Magee, *Technical Analysis of Stock Trends* (John Magee Inc., Springfield, Massachusetts, 1948)

Many popular trading strategies buy on countertrend declines in an uptrend and sell short on countertrend rallies in a downtrend. Buying declines in an uptrend means buying low relative to recent prices, selling short on rallies in a downtrend means selling high relative to recent prices. The concept makes sense because markets don't go straight up or straight down for very long, fluctuating instead in a zigzag series of impulse waves and corrective waves. Waves in the direction of the trend are impulse waves, and waves against the direction of the trend are corrective waves. In other words, in an uptrend, the upward waves are impulse waves, and the downward waves are corrective waves; in a downtrend, the downward waves are impulse waves, and the upward waves are corrective waves. In an uptrend (see Figure 4.1), the upward waves are generally longer in duration and larger in magnitude than the downward waves, whereas in a downtrend (see Figure 4.2), the downward waves generally last longer and move farther than the upward waves.

My *First Prize* strategy buys after a downward corrective wave in an uptrend when the uptrend resumes and sells

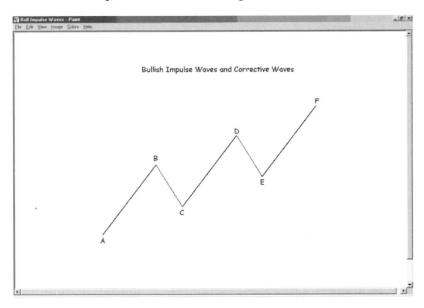

Figure 4.1   In this uptrend, waves A–B, C–D, and E–F are impulse waves. Waves B–C and D–E are corrective waves.

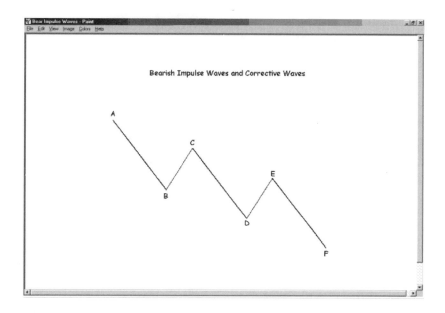

Figure 4.2 In this downtrend, waves A–B, C–D, and
E–F are impulse waves. Waves B–C and D–E are
corrective waves.

short after an upward corrective rally in a downtrend
when the downtrend resumes. Although a major trend
can include several corrective waves, *First Prize* only
trades the first decline in an uptrend and the first rally in
a downtrend: The first corrective wave offers the highest
probability of a winning trade. The odds for success de-
crease on subsequent corrective waves in the same trend.
(My *R2D2* strategy, which I describe later in this book, is
based on a special pattern that can form during corrective
waves after the first one, but that's the exception.)

First Prize employs the following technical tools: Japanese candlestick charts (or bar charts), swing highs and

29

swing lows, true range, average true range (ATR), break-outs to new highs and new lows, exponential moving averages (EMAs), moving average convergence-divergence (MACD), the directional movement index spread (DMI spread), the parabolic, and Fibonacci retracements. *R2D2* and *Triple Play* (the other strategies in this book) also use most of these technical tools. For readers who are unfamiliar with these tools, a brief explanation of each one follows.

Japanese Candlestick Charts

Although the Japanese have analyzed markets with candlestick charts since the early 1700s, their charts didn't become known in the West until 1991, when Steve Nison explained the charting method in his book, *Japanese Candlestick Charting Techniques* (New York Institute of Finance, 1991). Since then, candlesticks have become very popular in the West, enticing many technical analysts away from their familiar bar charts (see Figures 4.3 and 4.4) and toward the unfamiliar but beguiling candles.

Since candlestick charts (see Figure 4.5) depict exactly the same information as bar charts—open, high, low, and close—why have they become so quickly and widely accepted in the West? I think there are two main reasons: First, candlesticks are much more visually appealing and easier to read than bar charts, and second, candlesticks offer many useful, "new" patterns (discovered and refined over centuries in the East) that can be added to the Western technician's repertoire.

30

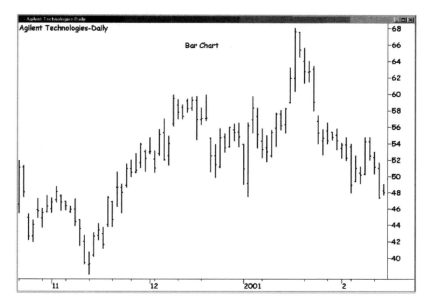

Figure 4.3   Each bar shows the open, high, low, and close of one day of trading. The extremes of each bar represent the daily highs and lows. The tick marks to the left and right of each bar represent the opens and closes, respectively.

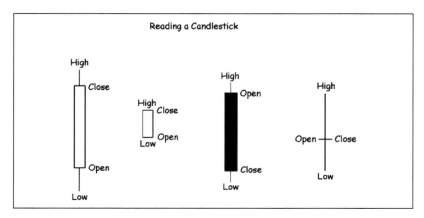

Figure 4.4   Reading a candlestick.

Figure 4.5 Each candle shows the open, high, low, and close of one day of trading. The white candles represent days when the close was above the open. The black candles represent days when the close was below the open. The thin lines at the tops and bottoms of the candles represent the daily highs and lows.

Most Japanese candlestick lines consist of two parts: a *real body* and its *shadows*. The real body represents the distance between a trading session's open and close, whereas the shadows represent the session's high and low. The real body of a candle is its thick part; the shadows are the thin lines drawn above and below the real body. When a stock closes above its open, the candle's real body is white (or hollow), and, when a stock closes below its open, the candle's real body is black (or filled). Thus, a white real body signifies upward price movement between the open

32

and the close, whereas a black real body signifies downward price movement between the open and the close. An upper shadow (a thin line extending above the real body) represents the market's high for the session; a lower shadow (a thin line extending below the real body) represents the market's low for the session.

The Japanese candlestick patterns that I find most useful in my *First Prize* strategy and the other strategies in this book include the following: belt-hold line, dark cloud cover and piercing line, doji, engulfing line, hammer and hanging man, inverted hammer and shooting star, harami and harami cross, morning star and evening star, tweezers, and windows. These candlestick patterns are described next. Note that I show the patterns at the end of corrective waves, not at the end of impulse waves. Candlestick patterns don't always do a very good job of signaling reversals of impulse waves and the beginnings of major new trends, but they do an excellent job of signaling the end of corrective waves and the resumption of the underlying trend. When you study the diagrams of the candlestick patterns, remember that the long diagonal line represents the direction of the impulse wave and that the short diagonal line represents the direction of the corrective wave. The bearish patterns are shown at the top of upward corrective waves within downtrends, and the bullish patterns are shown at the bottom of downward corrective waves within uptrends. The 38.2% and 61.8% labels in Figure 4.6 refer to Fibonacci retracement levels, discussed later in this book. For now, it's enough to know that the numbers identify the price levels at which the corrective waves have retraced 38.2% and 61.8% of the impulse waves.

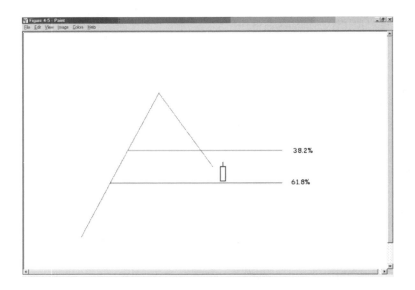

Figure 4.6   Bullish belt-hold line.

Belt-Hold Line

A bullish belt-hold line is a tall, white candle that opened at its low for the session; thus, it has no lower shadow. A bearish belt-hold line (see Figure 4.7) is a tall, black candle that opened at its session high, so it has no upper shadow.

Piercing Line and Dark Cloud Cover

A piercing line (see Figure 4.8) follows a tall, black candle in a downward wave. It opens below the previous candle's low but closes at least halfway into the previous

34

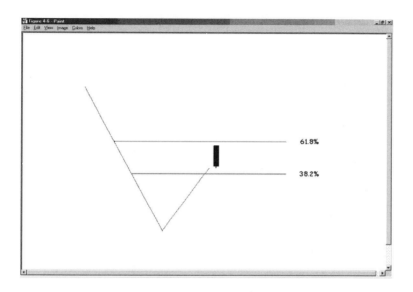

Figure 4.7   Bearish belt-hold line.

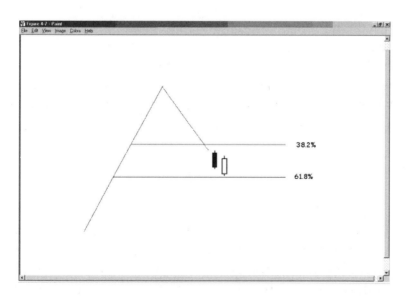

Figure 4.8   Piercing line.

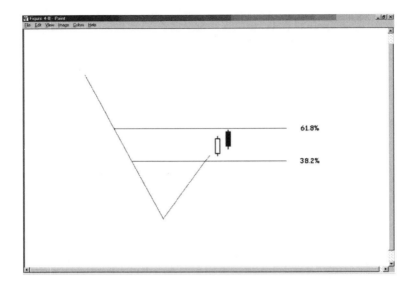

Figure 4.9   Dark cloud cover.

candle's real body. A dark cloud cover (see Figure 4.9), which follows a tall, white candle in an upward wave, opens above the previous candle's high but closes at least halfway into the previous candle's real body. A piercing line is bullish, and a dark cloud cover is bearish.

Doji

A doji represents a trading session in which the open and close occur at the same (or almost the same) price; therefore, a doji has no real body (or a very small real body). In a downward wave (see Figure 4.10), a doji is bullish, while in an upward wave, it's bearish (see Figure 4.11).

36

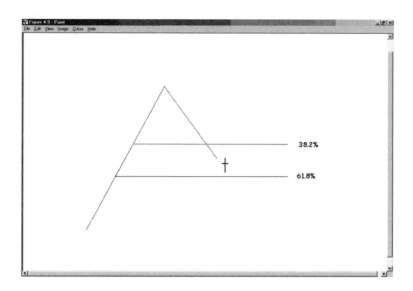

Figure 4.10   Bullish doji.

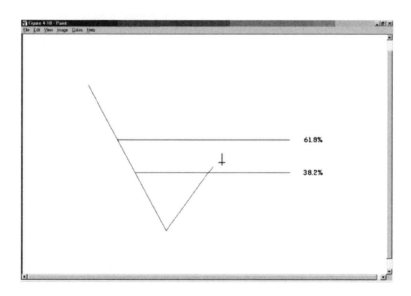

Figure 4.11   Bearish doji.

37

Engulfing Line

A bullish engulfing line (see Figure 4.12), which occurs in a downward wave, is a tall, white real body that engulfs the previous session's smaller, black real body. The bullish engulfing line opens below the previous session's close and closes above the previous session's open. A bearish engulfing line (see Figure 4.13) occurs in an upward wave. Its tall, black real body engulfs the previous session's smaller, white real body. In other words, a bearish engulfing line opens above the previous session's close and closes below the previous session's open. A bullish engulfing line often occurs at the end of a down-

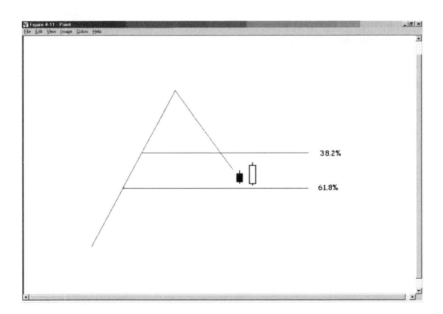

Figure 4.12   Bullish engulfing line.

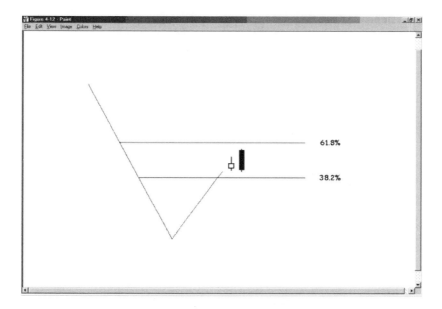

Figure 4.13 Bearish engulfing line.

ward corrective wave in an uptrend, and a bearish engulfing line often appears at the end of an upward corrective wave in a downtrend.

Hammer and Hanging Man

A hammer (see Figure 4.14), which occurs in a downward wave, has a small real body (either black or white)
at the top of its range. A hammer has little or no upper
shadow, but its lower shadow must be at least twice as
tall as the real body. A hanging man (see Figure 4.15) is
identical to a hammer, with one exception: A hanging

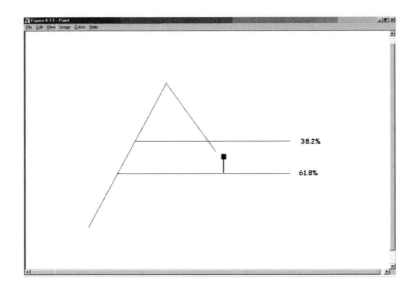

Figure 4.14   Hammer.

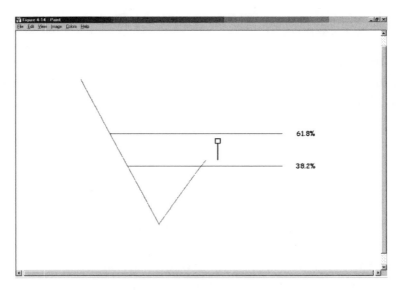

Figure 4.15   Hanging man.

man is found in an upward wave, whereas a hammer is found in a downward wave. A hammer is bullish; a hanging man is bearish.

Inverted Hammer and Shooting Star

An inverted hammer (see Figure 4.16), which occurs in a downward wave, is identical to a hammer, except that it's upside down (i.e., its small real body is at the bottom of its range). A shooting star (see Figure 4.17) is identical to an inverted hammer, but it is found in an upward wave. An inverted hammer is bullish if prices rally above its high within a few days, and a shooting star is bearish if prices decline below its low within a few days.

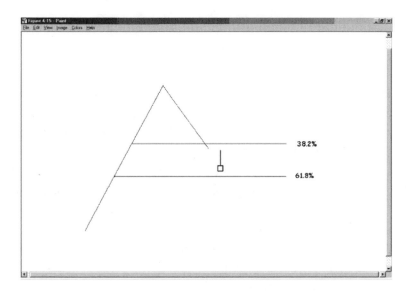

Figure 4.16   Inverted hammer.

41

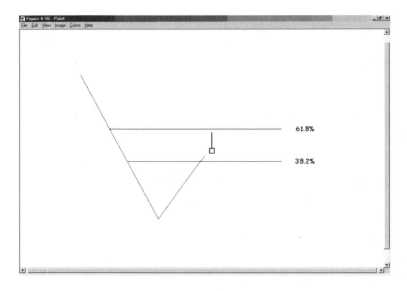

Figure 4.17 Shooting star.

Harami and Harami Cross

A harami (see Figures 4.18 and 4.19) is a small real body that is within the previous candle's real body. In other words, the previous candle engulfs the current session's candle. Although the color of the harami's real body is usually the opposite color of the previous candle, it may be either white or black. A harami cross is a combination of a harami and a doji; that is, its real body, which represents an open and close at the same or nearly the same price, is contained within the previous candle's real body. The harami and the harami cross are bullish (see Figure 4.20) in a downward wave and bearish (see Figure 4.21) in an upward wave.

42

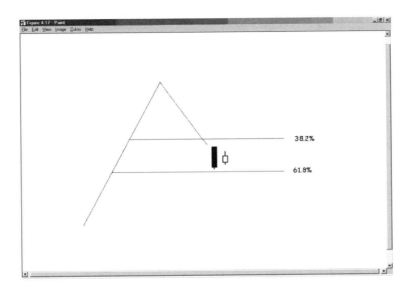

Figure 4.18   Bullish harami.

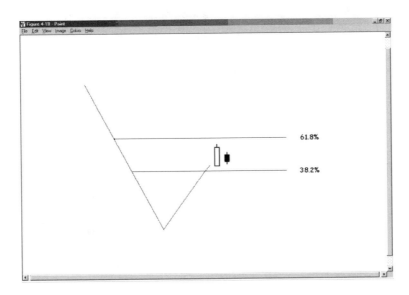

Figure 4.19   Bearish harami.

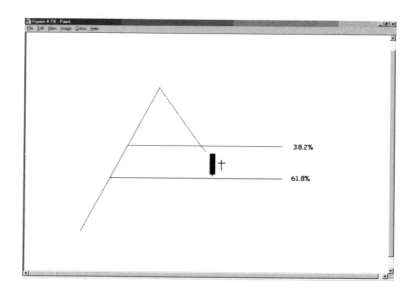

Figure 4.20   Bullish harami cross.

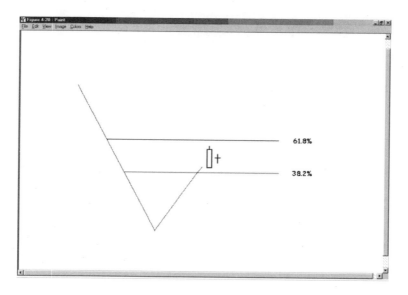

Figure 4.21   Bearish harami cross.

44

Morning Star and Evening Star

A morning star (see Figure 4.22), which occurs in a downward wave, consists of three candles: a tall, black real body; a small real body (either white or black) that gaps open below the real body of the first candle; and a tall, white candle with a strong close at least halfway into the first candle's real body. An evening star (see Figure 4.23) is a three-candle pattern in an upward wave: a tall, white real body; a small real body (either white or black) that gaps open above the real body of the first candle; and a tall, black candle with a close at least halfway into the first candle's real body. A morning star is bullish; an evening star is bearish.

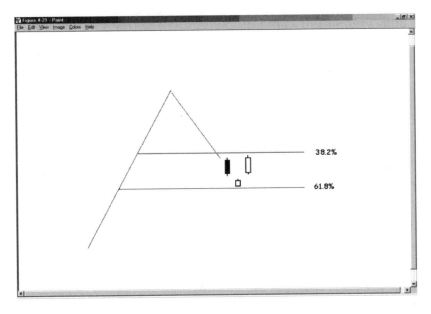

Figure 4.22 Morning star.

45

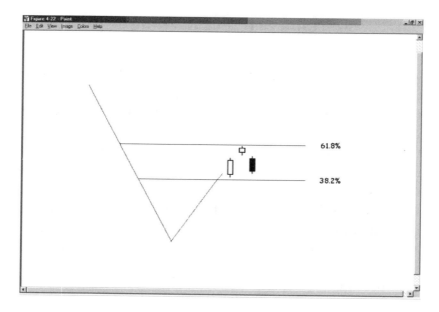

Figure 4.23   Evening star.

Tweezer Bottom and Tweezer Top

A tweezer bottom (see Figure 4.24) consists of two candles with the same (or nearly the same) high. A tweezer
top (see Figure 4.25) consists of two candles with the
same (or nearly the same) highs. For both tweezer bottoms and tweezer tops, the candles can either be adjacent
or a few candles apart. A tweezer bottom suggests short-
term support (a minor floor beneath the market), and a
tweezer top suggests short-term resistance (a minor ceiling above the market).

46

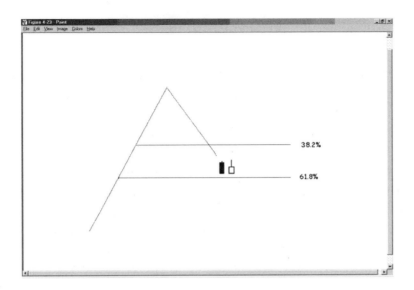

Figure 4.24 Tweezer bottom.

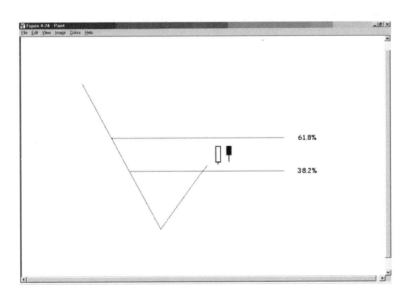

Figure 4.25 Tweezer top.

47

Windows

Windows are the Japanese candlestick equivalent of the bar chart's gap. A bullish window (see Figure 4.26) occurs when the current candle's low does not overlap the previous candle's high; a bearish window (see Figure 4.27) occurs when the current candle's high does not overlap the previous candle's low. A bullish window in a downward corrective wave can signal a resumption of an uptrend, whereas a bearish window in an upward corrective wave can signal a resumption of a downtrend.

Having completed our discussion of Japanese candlestick patterns, we will proceed to brief explanations of

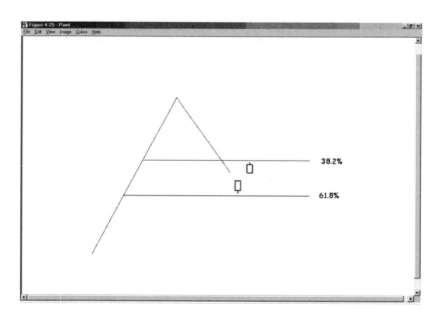

Figure 4.26 Bullish window.

48

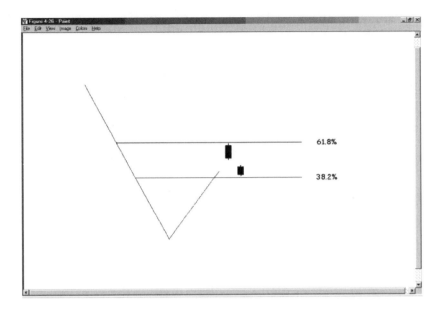

Figure 4.27 Bearish window.

several other components of *First Prize* and the other strategies in this book.

Swing Highs and Lows

Swing highs and swing lows (see Figure 4.28) often indicate levels of support and resistance (support is like a floor beneath the market; resistance is like a ceiling above the market). Swing highs and lows occur with different strengths: A swing high with a strength of one, for example, has at least one lower high to its immediate left and right, whereas a swing low with a strength of two

49

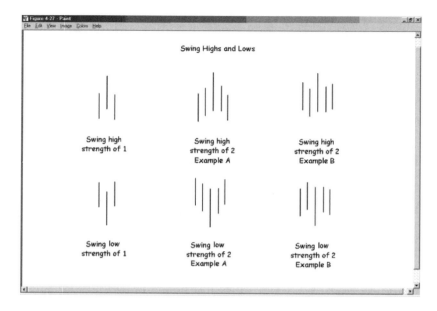

Figure 4.28 The swing high to the strength of one has one lower high to its left and right, and the swing low to the strength of one has one higher low to its left and right. The swing high to the strength of two has two lower highs to its left and right, and the swing low to the strength of two has two higher lows to its left and right. Note the acceptable variations of the pattern in the two example Bs above.

has at least two higher lows to its immediate left and right. When there is a different number of lower highs or higher lows to the left of a swing point than to the right of the point, the strength is equal to the lesser number. For example, if a swing high has three lower highs to its left and two lower highs to its right, the swing high has a strength of two; if a swing low has one higher low to its left and five higher lows to its right, the swing low has a strength of one.

True Range

A market's true range (see Figure 4.29) is the largest of the following: today's high minus today's low, today's high minus yesterday's close, or yesterday's close minus

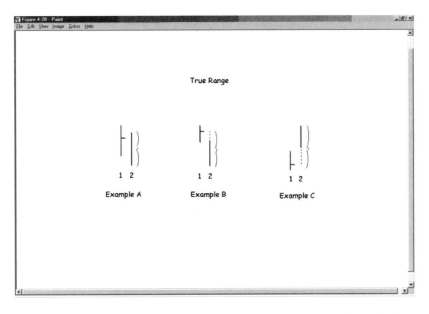

Figure 4.29 In Example A, the true range is today's high minus today's low. In Example B, the true range is yesterday's close minus today's low. In Example C, the true range is today's high minus yesterday's close.

today's low. In other words, if today's price bar (or candle) doesn't overlap yesterday's close, true range fills in the gap.

Average True Range

An average true range (ATR) (see Figure 4.30) is a simple moving average of the true range. In *First Prize*, I use a 21-day ATR.

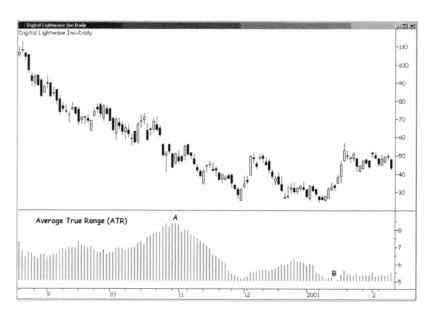

Figure 4.30 The 21-day average true range (ATR) is plotted in the lower window. In this example, the ATR ranged from a high of $8.40 at point A to a low of $5.50 at point B.

Price Channels

A price channel (see Figure 4.31) consists of the highest high and lowest low of a specified number of days. Breakouts from price channels often portend significant price trends in the direction of the breakout.

Figure 4.31 This Japanese candlestick chart includes a 21-day price channel. The dots on the highs and lows of some candles indicate breakouts to new 21-day highs and lows.

Exponential Moving Averages

Technical analysts have created many types of moving averages—adaptive, exponential, simple, and weighted, to name just a few—but all moving averages perform the same function: smoothing data to make the trend easier to identify. Simple moving averages (SMAs) are, as their name suggests, the least complex type. To calculate a 10-day SMA of closing prices, for example, just add the last 10 closes and divide the total by 10. SMAs do smooth price data, of course, but, in my opinion, they have two shortcomings. First, SMAs assign equal weight to each data point: In a 200-day SMA of closing prices, for example, the close 200 days ago counts as much as the close today. I believe that the more recent data should be assigned greater weight. Second, SMAs abruptly drop "old" data when it falls outside the lookback period. In a 20-day SMA, for example, today's close is added to the SMA, and the close that is now 21 days old is dropped from the SMA. Abruptly dropping the old data sometimes results in an SMA line that rises or declines sharply on days when the most recent closes are very similar or even identical. This aberration occurs when the closing price that is dropped from the calculation is significantly higher or lower than the current close—drop a much lower close and the SMA leaps up; drop a much higher close and the SMA takes a dive.

Exponential moving averages (EMAs) (see Figure 4.32) solve both problems of the SMA (i.e., they assign more weight to recent data and don't abruptly drop old data). For example, if you have 1,000 days of data for a stock and calculate a 21-day EMA of closing prices, the

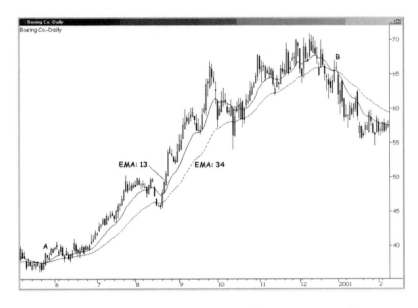

Figure 4.32 The solid line is a 13-day exponential moving average (EMA). The dotted line is a 34-day EMA. When EMA:13 is above EMA:34, the trend is up. When EMA:13 is below EMA:34, the trend is down. Point A marks the beginning of a new uptrend. Point B marks the beginning of a new downtrend.

EMA includes all 1,000 days in its calculation, but it gives greater weight to the most recent data and less weight to the data farther back in time. The number of days specified for the EMA (21 in this example) determines how much weight is given to today's close and how much weight is given to the previous day's EMA. Since you won't have to calculate EMAs by hand—your technical analysis software calculates them for you in one or two seconds—I won't elaborate on the math. In *First Prize*, I rely on two EMAs—a fast one and a slow one—to keep me on the right side of the trend, buying only when the fast EMA exceeds the slow EMA and selling short only when the fast EMA is less than the slow one.

Moving Average Convergence-Divergence

The MACD (see Figure 4.33), which was developed by Gerald Appel in the late 1970s, integrates positive features of both momentum indicators and trend-following indicators; that is, it measures the rate of acceleration or deceleration of price changes without forfeiting its ability to keep pace with a trending market. The MACD indicator consists of two lines and a histogram. The MACD line is the difference between a fast EMA and a slow EMA. The signal line is an EMA of the MACD line. When the fast EMA is greater than the slow EMA, the MACD line is positive (i.e., greater than zero); when the fast EMA is less than the slow EMA, the MACD line is negative (i.e., less than zero). The MACD histogram is the difference between the MACD line and the signal line. It's drawn as a series of vertical bars that fluctuate above and below zero. When the MACD line is above the signal line, the MACD histogram is positive (i.e., greater than zero); when the MACD line is below the signal line, the MACD histogram is negative (i.e., less than zero).

For *First Prize*, *R2D2*, and *Triple Play*, I use a three-day EMA for the fast average, an eight-day EMA for the slow average, and a 13-day EMA for the signal line.

56

Figure 4.33 The solid line in the top window is a three-day exponential moving average (EMA). The dotted line in the top window is an eight-day EMA. The solid line in the bottom window is the MACD line: the difference between EMA:3 and EMA:8. When EMA:3 is greater than EMA:8, the MACD line is greater than zero. When EMA:3 is less than EMA:8, the MACD line is less than zero. The vertical bars in the bottom window are the MACD histogram (the difference between the MACD line and the signal line). When the MACD line is greater than the signal line, the histogram is greater than zero. When the MACD line is less than the signal line, the histogram is less than zero.

Directional Movement Index

Welles Wilder introduced the directional movement index (DMI) in his 1978 classic, *New Concepts in Technical Trading Systems*. The DMI (see Figure 4.34) is composed of

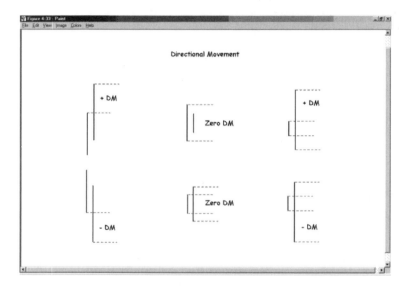

Figure 4.34 *Directional movement* (DM) is the largest part of today's range that is outside yesterday's range. If today's range extends above yesterday's range, directional movement is positive; if today's range extends below yesterday's range, directional movement is negative. If today's range is within yesterday's range, or if today's range extends above and below yesterday's range by equal amounts, directional movement for the day is zero. If today's range extends both above and below yesterday's range but by unequal amounts, directional movement for the day is positive if the extension *above* yesterday's range is larger and negative if the extension *below* yesterday's range is larger.

58

two lines: the positive directional index (+DI), which measures the amount of positive (upward) directional movement over a specified number of days, and the minus directional index (–DI), which measures the negative (downward) directional movement over the same period. The DMI spread (see Figure 4.35) is simply the difference between +DI and –DI. A DMI spread of +15 or higher indicates a strong uptrend; a DMI spread of –15 or lower signals a strong downtrend. In *First Prize*, I rely on the DMI spread to identify impulse waves that are trending steadily, as opposed to those exhibiting less consistent directional movement.

Parabolic Indicator

Welles Wilder named his parabolic indicator (see Figure 4.36) for the curving shape its dots usually form when plotted on a chart—a *parabola*. Wilder presented the parabolic as a stop-and-reverse indicator. In other words, a trader would always have a position in the market. He would exit a short position and buy (go long) on a buy signal; he would exit a long position and sell short on a sell signal. In this book's three strategies, I rely on the parabolic as one of several possible ways to exit a trade, but I don't use it to enter a new trade.

When the parabolic gives a buy signal, a new series of dots begins at the low of the most recent downtrend. The dots rise every day, but they rise slowly at first, giving the trade some room and time to develop properly.

Figure 4.35 Directional movement index (DMI) and DMI spread. The solid line in the middle window is the +DI (the amount of positive directional movement), and the dotted line is the −DI (negative directional movement). At point A, +DI crosses above −DI, indicating overall positive directional movement. At point B, +DI dips below −DI for one day but rises back above −DI the next day. At point C, −DI crosses above +DI, remaining there for the remainder of the chart, indicating overall negative directional movement for that period. In the bottom window, the histogram represents the DMI spread (i.e., the difference between +DI and −DI). The histogram's crossings of the zero line correspond to the crossings of +DI and −DI in the middle window. When the DMI spread rises to +15 or higher, the market is in a strong uptrend. When the DMI spread declines to −15 or lower, the market is in a strong downtrend.

Figure 4.36 The market declines to the rising parabolic dot at point B. A new series of dots begins at point C at the price level equal to the previous uptrend's high at point A. The dots after point C decline every day, slowly at first, then faster as the downtrend makes new lows. At point E, prices hit the parabolic, signaling a buy. The new series of dots begins on the day after point E at the price level of the point D low. The new uptrend never really takes off, and the parabolic gives a timely sell signal at point F.

As the market makes new highs, an acceleration factor is added to the calculation of the indicator, and the dots rise faster to lock in more profits. Eventually, the market hits the parabolic stop, signaling an exit from the trade. After giving a sell signal, the new series of dots begins at the high of the most recent uptrend. The dots fall slowly at first, but as the market makes new lows, they fall more rapidly. When the downtrend loses momentum, the parabolic usually gives a timely signal to exit the trade.

Fibonacci Retracements

In his book *Liber Abaci/The Book of Calculations*, Leonardo Fibonacci, a thirteenth-century Italian mathematician, popularized the intriguing number sequence that bears his name. Many traders believe that the Fibonacci number series generates important mathematical ratios that can be incorporated into their trading strategies. The Fibonacci number series begins 1, 1, 2, 3, 5, 8, 13, 21, 34, 55, 89 and extends infinitely. Following are three of the many unique characteristics of the Fibonacci series.

1. The next number in the series is always the sum of the two previous numbers (e.g., 13 plus 21 equals 34).
2. The ratio of any number in the series to the next higher number approximates 0.618 after the first four numbers (e.g., 13 divided by 21 equals 0.619).

This ratio gets closer to 0.618 as the numbers in the series increase (e.g., 144 divided by 233 equals 0.618).

3. The ratio of any number in the sequence to the next lower number approximates 1.618 after the first four numbers (e.g., 34 divided by 21 equals 1.619). This ratio gets closer to 1.618 as the numbers increase (e.g., 377 divided by 233 equals 1.618).

The ratios generated by the Fibonacci number series were recognized in other cultures and times as the *golden ratio* or *golden mean*. The ancient Egyptians, Greeks, and Romans used these ratios in their art, architecture, mathematics, music, and science. The golden ratio figures prominently in the Great Pyramid at Giza and the Parthenon in Athens. Among the artifacts left by Pythagoras, one of the ancient world's greatest mathematicians and philosophers, is his drawing of a triangle based on these ratios that he labeled, "The Secret of the Universe." Leonardo da Vinci used the ratios in his masterpieces, the *Last Supper* and the *Mona Lisa*. The ratios also appear frequently in nature: The human inner ear, the chambered nautilus shell, the rows of seeds on a sunflower head, and even the expanding patterns of spiral galaxies all exhibit Fibonacci ratios.

Fibonacci ratios are as prevalent and influential in the financial markets as they are in many other human creations and in nature. Many traders who include Fibonacci ratios in their market analysis look for 38.2% or 61.8% retracements of impulse waves and buy or sell at those levels. They buy at a 38.2% or a 61.8% retracement of a bullish impulse wave, expecting support at those levels, and they sell short at a 38.2% or a 61.8% retracement of a bearish impulse wave, expecting resistance. In *First Prize*, I use Fibonacci ratios differently. I look for retracements that are at least 38.2% but not more than 61.8% of the impulse wave rather than looking for retracements that end specifically at 38.2% or 61.8% of the impulse wave. To establish these retracement zones, I must be able to identify the beginning and ending points of the impulse waves. Finding the ending point is easy: In an uptrend it's the current 21-day high, and in a downtrend it's the current 21-day low. Finding the beginning of an impulse wave, however, can be tricky. Usually, the most recent 21-day low marks the beginning of a bullish impulse wave (see Figure 4.37), and the most recent 21-day high marks the beginning of a bearish impulse wave (see Figure 4.38). However, sometimes other lows and highs seem more logical and more appropriate.

When the 21-day high or low doesn't stand out as the most prominent point for the start of the impulse wave, I turn to the MACD indicator to help me identify the beginning of the impulse wave. In an uptrend, the MACD line's crossing from above the signal line to below it signals a retracement, and the previous MACD crossing from below the signal line to above it sometimes identifies the best candidate for the starting point of the impulse wave. The starting point in this case is the swing

Figure 4.37 Finding the beginning of a bullish impulse wave. The breakout to a new 21-day low at point X is clearly not the logical starting point for the impulse wave that ended at point B. In cases like this, I turn to the MACD for help. The MACD line's crossing of the signal line at point 2 is a *downward* crossing, signaling the beginning of a corrective wave. Look to the left of point 2 and find the MACD line's most recent *upward* crossing of the signal line (point 1 in this example). The upward crossing at point 1 corresponds to point A on the candlestick chart—a much more logical beginning for the impulse wave.

Figure 4.38   Finding the beginning of a bearish impulse wave. The breakout to a new 21-day high at point X is not a logical starting point for the impulse wave that ended at point B. The (MACD) line's (solid line) crossing of the signal line at point 2 is an *upward* crossing, signaling the beginning of a corrective wave. Look to the left of point 2 and find the MACD line's most recent *downward* crossing of the signal line (dashed line) (point 1 in this example). The downward crossing at point 1 identifies the correct beginning of the impulse wave: The closest swing high to point 1 is point A on the candlestick chart.

low (a low with a higher low on each side of it) nearest to the upward MACD crossing of the signal line. In a downtrend, the MACD line's crossing from below the signal line to above it signals a retracement, and the previous MACD crossing from above the signal line to below it sometimes pinpoints the impulse wave's most likely starting point. In this case, the swing high (a high with a lower high on each side) nearest to the downward MACD crossing of the signal line is the starting point (see Figures 4.39 and 4.40).

Figure 4.39 Bullish Fibonacci retracement. Point A marks the beginning of the impulse wave, and point B marks its end. Point C is the low of the corrective wave. Note that point C is in the Fibonacci retracement zone, that is, between a 38.2% and a 61.8% retracement of the impulse wave.

Figure 4.40 Bearish Fibonacci retracement. The impulse wave begins at point A and extends to point B. The corrective wave stops at the 61.8% retracement level at point C.

First Prize: The Rules

To trade the *First Prize* strategy, you'll need the following technical tools: a Japanese candlestick chart (or a bar chart), 13-day and 34-day EMAs, a 13-day DMI spread, a 3-8-13 MACD, and a 21-day ATR. The setup, entry, and exits for *First Prize* follow.

Trading the Long Side

Setup

1. EMA:13 is greater than EMA:34.
2. The market makes a new 21-day high, suggesting that the current price swing is an impulse wave.
3. The DMI spread is greater than 15 on the day the market makes its most recent 21-day high, thereby confirming the impulse wave.
4. Today's close is between a 38.2% and a 61.8% retracement of the impulse wave.
5. The MACD line crosses below the signal line for the first time since the signal line crossed above zero, and the signal line remains above zero.
6. The MACD histogram is rising (i.e., it's greater than it was yesterday).
7. Although not required, a bullish Japanese candlestick pattern can provide additional confirmation of a high-probability setup.

Entry

Buy tomorrow above today's high. (In my *First Prize* strategies, *above* the high means any small amount above the high (e.g., 12 cents for a stock or one tick for a commodity), and *below* the low means any small amount below the low).

Exits

1. When your buy order is filled, place an initial protective stop below the low of the corrective wave.

69

2. As prices rise, trail a stop (raise the stop) to lock in some profits while still giving the market some room to run.

Trading the Short Side

Setup

1. EMA:13 is less than EMA:34.
2. The market makes a new 21-day low, suggesting that the current price swing is an impulse wave.
3. The DMI spread is less than −15 on the day the market makes its most recent 21-day low, thereby confirming the impulse wave.
4. Today's close is between a 38.2% and a 61.8% retracement of the impulse wave.
5. The MACD line crosses above the signal line for the first time since the signal line crossed below zero, and the signal line remains below zero.
6. The MACD histogram is declining (i.e., it's less than it was yesterday).
7. Although not required, a bearish Japanese candlestick pattern can provide additional confirmation of a high-probability setup.

Entry

Sell short tomorrow below today's low.

Exits

1. When your sell order is filled, place an initial protective stop above the high of the corrective wave.
2. As prices fall, trail a stop (lower the stop) to lock in some profits while still giving the market some room to run.

A note about exits: In the following examples, I'll show you a wide variety of techniques that can be used to exit from *First Prize* and the other strategies in this book. For each trade, I selected an exit that worked very well in that particular example. In most cases, there was probably an exit technique that would have worked even better than the one I chose, and there were others that would not have worked as well. As you study these trades, please spend some time learning the various exit techniques I've presented. Then choose a few of the techniques that you like best and study how they would have performed in each of the trades. Your objective should be to become a specialist in one or two of the exit techniques that make the most sense to you and that you feel very comfortable with. Because exits are at least as important as any other component of a trading strategy, you will be well rewarded for the time you spend focusing on your exit techniques.

Figure 4.41 is a daily chart of AFLAC Inc (AFL). The impulse wave begins at point A, the lowest low in the past 21 days, and continues to point B, the highest high in 21 days. The DMI spread is greater than 15 at point 4.

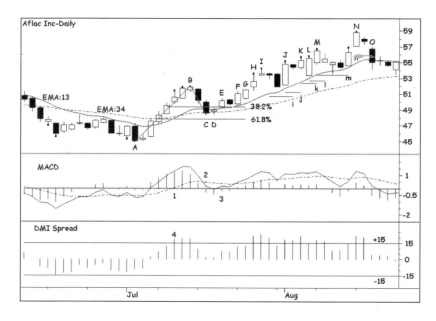

Figure 4.41 Aflac Inc.

The MACD's signal line crosses above zero at point 1, and EMA:13 crosses above EMA:34 one day later. The MACD line crosses below the signal line at point 2, and the MACD histogram turns up at point 3. Candle C, which falls within the Fibonacci retracement zone, marks the end of the corrective wave, and candle D is a harami. Buy on candle E above the high of the harami, and set your initial protective stop below the low of candle C.

In this example, let's trail a stop at the highest closing price of the trade minus two times the ATR on the day before entry. The ATR at point D is 1.46, and $2 \times 1.46 =$ 2.92. At point F, the close (51.06) minus twice the ATR (2.92) gives us a stop of 48.14. At point G, the close

(51.56) minus 2.92 raises the stop to 48.64. At point H, the stop rises to 49.70, at point I to 50.70, and at point J to 51.26. At point K the stop moves up to 52.39, at point L to 52.64, and at point M to 53.50. Point N turns out to be the highest close of the trade (58.81), and 58.81 minus 2.92 places the final stop at 55.89, which is hit at point O.

Figure 4.42 is a daily chart of Southtrust Corp (SOTR). The impulse wave begins at point A, which is not a new 21-day low. The 21-day low prior to point A is too far away to be relevant to the upswing. To find a more appropriate and logical point A, I turned to the MACD indicator. The MACD line's crossing of the signal line at

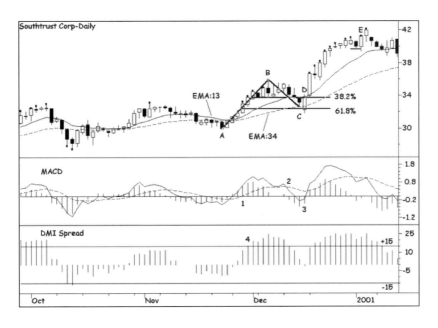

Figure 4.42   Southtrust Corp.

point 2 (signaling a retracement) was a downward crossing, so I looked to the left of point 2 until I found the MACD line's most recent upward crossing of the signal line, which was two days before point 1. The best choice for point A in this example is the swing low four days before point 1. Point B marks the high of the impulse wave, a new 21-day high, and candle C closes in the Fibonacci retracement zone. The DMI spread is greater than 15 at point 4. EMA:13 is greater than EMA:34, and the MACD's signal line is greater than zero at point 1. The MACD line crosses below the signal line at point 2, and the MACD histogram rises at point 3.

Buy on candle D above the previous candle's high. Candle D turns out to be a bullish engulfing line, thus providing additional confirmation for the trade. Set your initial protective stop below the low of candle D, the low of the corrective wave. In this example, let's use a five-day trailing stop; in other words, let's exit when prices fall below the lowest low of the last five days. The trailing stop is hit on candle E.

Figure 4.43 is a daily chart of Hartford Financial Services Group (HIG). The impulse wave begins at point A, a new 21-day high, and ends at point B, a new 21-day low. EMA:13 is less than EMA:34, and the MACD's signal line is less than zero at point 1. The MACD line crosses above the signal line at point 2, and the MACD histogram declines at point 3. The DMI spread falls below −15 at point 4. Candle C posts the high of the corrective wave in the Fibonacci retracement zone. Sell short on candle D below the previous candle's low and set your initial protective stop above the high of candle C.

74

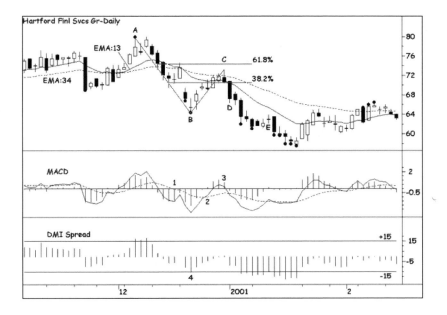

Figure 4.43   Hartford Financial Services Group.

Figure 4.44 shows an example of another way you can trail a stop: The initial risk on the trade is $3.39 per share. The first target is a close less than the entry price minus the initial risk (70.11 − 3.39 = 66.72), which occurs on candle E. Move the stop to breakeven (70.11). The second target is a close less than target 1 minus the initial risk (66.72 − 3.39 = 63.33), which occurs on candle F. Move the stop to target 2 (63.33). The third target is target 2 (63.33) minus the initial risk (3.39) = 59.94, which occurs on candle G. The fourth target is 56.55 (59.94

Figure 4.44 HIG targets and exits.

minus 3.39), but prices rally to 59.94, stopping out the trade before it reaches target 4.

Figure 4.45, a daily chart of Time Warner, Inc. (TWX), shows another example of selling short. The impulse wave begins at point A, a new 21-day high, and ends at point B, a new 21-day low. The high of the corrective wave is on candle C in the Fibonacci retracement zone. The DMI spread declines below –15 at point 4. EMA:13 is less than EMA:34, and the MACD's signal line is less than zero at point 1. The MACD line crosses above the signal line at point 2, and the MACD histogram declines at point 3. Sell short on candle D below the low of candle C.

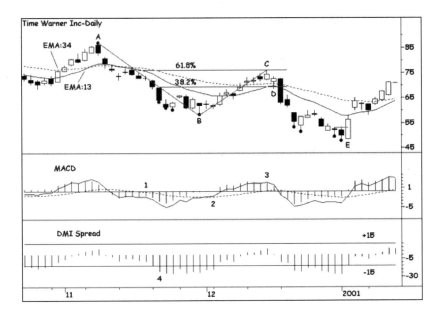

Figure 4.45   Time Warner, Inc.

The candle after D turns out to be a bearish belt-hold line, providing additional confirmation for the trade. Set your initial protective stop above the high of candle C. In this example, let's trail a three-day stop; in other words, we'll exit when prices rise above the highest high of the last three days. Exit on candle E, which turns out to be a bullish engulfing line and the low of the downtrend.

First Prize works as well in the futures markets as it does in the stock market. Figure 4.46 is a daily chart of municipal bond futures.

The market falls to a new 21-day low at point A and rises to a new 21-day high at point B. The MACD's signal

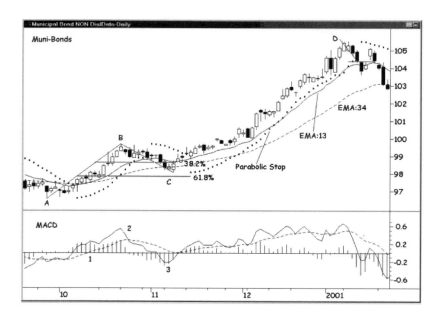

Figure 4.46 Municipal bonds.

line crosses above zero at point 1, and EMA:13 crosses above EMA:34 one day later. The MACD line crosses below the signal line at point 2, and the MACD histogram turns up at point 3. Buy on the day after candle C above candle C's high and set your initial protective stop below the low of the candle after C—the new low of the corrective wave.

In this example, let's use the parabolic indicator for our exit technique. Four days after candle C, the market hits the parabolic dots that were above recent prices, and a new series of dots appears below current prices. The new parabolic series begins at the low of the day after candle C (the low of the corrective wave) and rises every day. Finally, on candle D, the market declines to the parabolic dot, and we are stopped out of the trade.

Figure 4.47 is a daily chart of Canadian dollar futures. The impulse wave begins at point A, a new 21-day high, and ends at point B, a new 21-day low. EMA:13 is less than EMA:34, and the MACD's signal line is less than zero at point 1. The MACD line crosses above the signal line at point 2, and the MACD histogram declines at point 3. Candle C is a dark cloud cover in the Fibonacci

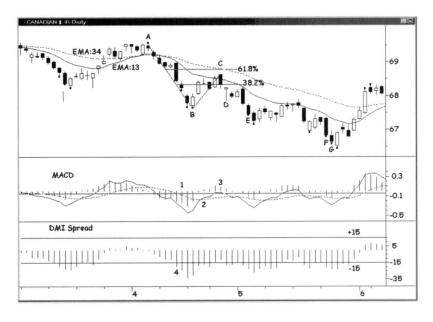

Figure 4.47 Canadian dollar.

retracement zone, implying that the corrective wave may be over. Sell short on candle D below the low of candle C and set your initial protective stop above the high of candle C. Beginning with this trade, let's add a breakeven stop to our exit strategy: When open profits on a closing basis are greater than the trade's initial risk, we'll lower the stop to breakeven. The risk on this trade is 46 ticks (in Canadian dollar futures, each tick is worth $10 per contract), so the first objective is .6773. Candle E closes below the first objective, so we lower the protective stop to breakeven (.6819).

Next I'd like to introduce a profit-target exit. Here's how to determine the target: First, subtract the impulse wave's low from its high (.6957 − .6764 = .0193). Second, multiply the size of the impulse wave by 0.618, one of the main Fibonacci ratios (193 × 0.618 = 119). Third, subtract .0119 from the high at point C (.6862 minus .0119 = .6743). The profit target is .6743, 61.8% of the previous impulse wave subtracted from the high of the corrective wave. After a close below the target (.6743), exit on the next day's open. Candle F closes at .6683, so we take our profits at the open of candle G.

Figure 4.48 is a weekly chart of Autodesk (ADSK). The impulse wave begins at point A, a new 21-day low, and continues to point B, a new 21-day high. The DMI spread is greater than 15 at point 4. The MACD's signal line crosses above zero at point 1, and EMA:13 crosses above EMA:34 seven weeks later. The MACD line crosses below the signal line at point 2, and the MACD histogram turns up at point 3. Candle C marks the end of

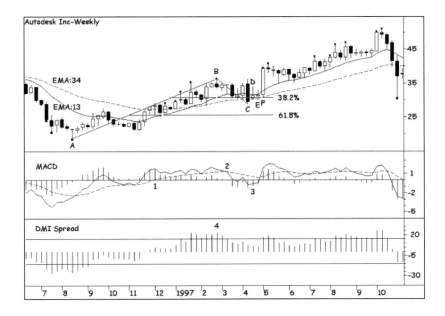

Figure 4.48   Autodesk Inc.

the corrective wave in the Fibonacci retracement zone, and the candle after C is a harami. Candle E doesn't exceed the high of D, but candle F does penetrate the high of candle E. Buy on candle F and set your initial protective stop below the low of candle C.

In this example, let's trail a parabolic stop. Figure 4.49 shows an exit on the candle marked X (for exit) when prices decline to the parabolic stop.

Figure 4.50 is a weekly chart of Allergan (AGN). The impulse wave begins at point A, a new 21-day high, and

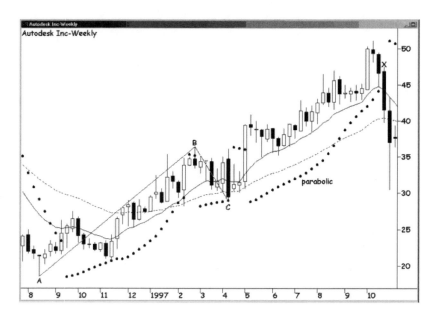

Figure 4.49 ADSK with parabolic stop.

ends at point B, a new 21-day low. The DMI spread declines below −15 at point 4. EMA:13 is less than EMA:34, and the MACD's signal line is less than zero at point 1. The MACD line crosses above the signal line at point 2, and the MACD histogram declines at point 3. Candle C marks the high of the corrective wave in the Fibonacci retracement zone, and candle D turns the MACD histogram down. The candle after D doesn't fall below candle D's low, so wait until candle E and sell short below the previous candle's low. Set your initial protective stop above the high of candle C. When open profits on a closing basis are greater than the trade's initial risk, lower the stop to breakeven. The risk on this trade is 0.93, so the

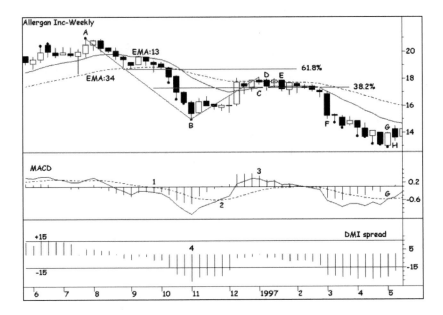

Figure 4.50 Allergan Inc.

first objective is 16.35 (the entry price of 17.28 − 0.93 = 16.35). At point F, the market closes at 15.25, well below the first objective, so lower the protective stop to break-even (17.28).

Let's use a simple and very aggressive exit technique on this trade. When the MACD line crosses above the signal line, exit the trade on the next candle's open. The crossover occurs on candle G, so cover the short position on the open of candle H.

Figure 4.51 is a five-minute chart of QQQ, the NAS-DAQ-100 Index tracking stock. QQQ, which trades just like an individual stock, actually represents a share in the portfolio of NASDAQ-100 stocks.

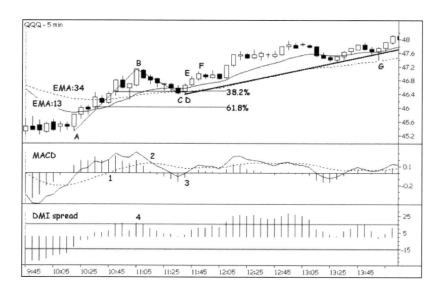

Figure 4.51   QQQ.

The impulse wave begins at point A, the lowest low in the past 21 periods and continues to point B, the highest high in 21 periods. The DMI spread is greater than 15 at point 4. The MACD's signal line crosses above zero at point 1, and EMA:13 crosses above EMA:34 three periods later. The MACD line crosses below the signal line at point 2, and the MACD histogram turns up at point 3. Candle C marks the low of the corrective wave in the Fibonacci retracement zone, and candle D turns the MACD histogram up. Buy on candle E above the high at D, and set your initial protective stop below the low of C. Goal 1 is a close equal to or greater than the entry price plus the amount of the initial risk on the trade (46.73 + 0.36 =

84

47.09). Candle F reaches the goal, so raise the stop to breakeven. On this trade, let's use a bullish trendline drawn from the swing low at D to the swing low six periods before G to signal our exit. On candle G, prices fall below the bullish trendline, so we exit the trade.

Figure 4.52 is another five-minute chart of QQQ. The impulse wave begins at point A, a new 21-period high, and ends at point B, a new 21-period low. EMA:13 is less than EMA:34, and the MACD's signal line is less than zero at point 1. The MACD line crosses above the signal line at point 2, and the MACD histogram declines at point 3. Candle C marks the high of the corrective wave in the Fibonacci retracement zone. Sell short on candle D

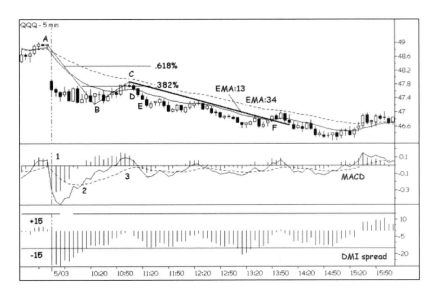

Figure 4.52   QQQ.

below the low of candle C and set your initial protective stop above the high of candle C. When open profits on a closing basis are greater than the trade's initial risk, lower the stop to breakeven. The risk on this trade is only 0.22, so the first objective is 47.47 (the entry price of 47.69 − 0.22 = 16.35). On candle E, the market closes at 47.36, so lower the protective stop to breakeven (47.69). Let's exit this trade on candle F on the penetration of the bearish trendline drawn from the swing high at C to the swing high 16 periods after C.

Figures 4.53 and 4.54 are weekly charts of unleaded gas futures. The impulse wave begins at point A, a new 21-week low, and continues to point B, a new 21-week

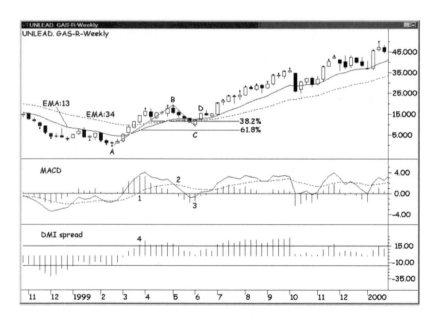

Figure 4.53 Unleaded gas.

Figure 4.54 Unleaded gas with exponential moving average exit.

high. The DMI spread is greater than +15 at point 4. The MACD's signal line crosses above zero at point 1, the MACD line crosses below the signal line at point 2, and the MACD histogram turns up at point 3. Candle C is a piercing line in the Fibonacci retracement zone. Buy on candle D above the high of candle C and set your initial protective stop below the low of candle C. When open profits on a closing basis are greater than the trade's initial risk, raise the stop to breakeven. The risk on this trade is 4.10, so the first objective is 17.15 (the entry price of 13.05 + 4.10 = 17.15). Three weeks after candle D, the market closes at 20.35, so raise the stop to breakeven (13.05). Figure 4.54 shows an exit when prices fall below the 34-week EMA. On candle F, prices penetrate the average, and we take our profits at 78.84.

Figure 4.55 is a weekly chart of wheat futures. The impulse wave begins at point A, a new 21-day high, and ends at point B, a new 21-day low. The DMI spread declines below −15 at point 4. EMA:13 is less than EMA:34, and the MACD's signal line is less than zero at point 1. The MACD line crosses above the signal line at point 2, and the MACD histogram declines at point 3. Candle C marks the high of the corrective wave in the Fibonacci retracement zone, and candle D turns the MACD histogram down. Sell short on the candle after D below can-

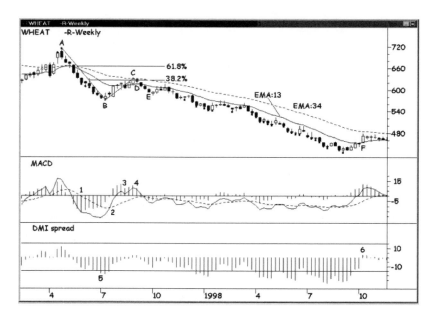

Figure 4.55   Wheat.

dle D's low and set your initial protective stop above the high of candle C. When open profits on a closing basis are greater than the trade's initial risk, lower the stop to breakeven. The risk on this trade is 19 cents per bushel (one contract equals 5,000 bushels), so the first objective is 598 3/4 (the entry price of 617 3/4 − 19 = 598 3/4). Candle E closes at 594, well below the first objective, so lower the protective stop to breakeven (617 3/4).

For this last example of a *First Prize* trade, let's take profits on the next open after the DMI spread crosses above zero. The crossover occurs on candle F, so cover the short position at 468 1/2, the next candle's open.

Summary

My *First Prize* strategy integrates technical indicators, Fibonacci retracement zones, Japanese candlestick patterns, an initial protective stop, and a variety of trailing stops to accomplish the following: (a) to enter a trade in the direction of the underlying trend after the first pullback, (b) to limit the trade's initial risk, and (c) to lock in some profits while still giving the market some room to run. The next strategy we'll study, *R2D2*, employs most of the same indicators and candlestick patterns as *First Prize*. The major difference between the two strategies is that *First Prize* trades only the first pullback of an impulse wave, whereas *R2D2* trades pullbacks that occur after the first one when a specific MACD pattern develops.

Chapter 4 Quiz

1. In an uptrend, the upward price swings are impulse waves, and the downward price swings are corrective waves.

   True   False

2. Impulse waves are usually shorter in duration and smaller in magnitude than corrective waves.

   True   False

3. The greater the number of corrective waves in a trend, the higher the probability for a winning trade.

   True   False

4. In Japanese candlestick charts, the real body represents the open and close, and the upper and lower shadows represent the high and low.

   True   False

5. On a daily candlestick chart, a white (or hollow) real body means that today's close was greater than yesterday's close; a black (or filled) real body means that today's close was less than yesterday's close.

   True   False

6. Candlestick patterns generally do a better job of signaling the resumption of an impulse wave than they do of signaling a major trend reversal.

   True   False

7. In *First Prize*, a corrective wave should retrace between 38.2% and 61.8% of the preceding impulse wave.

True   False

8. Support is like a ceiling above the current price, and resistance is like a floor below the current price.

True   False

9. A price low with three higher lows immediately before it and five higher lows immediately after it would be a swing low with a strength of eight.

True   False

10. If today's high is less than yesterday's close, today's true range is yesterday's close minus today's low.

True   False

11. If today's low is above yesterday's close, today's true range is today's high minus yesterday's low.

True   False

12. A new 21-day low usually indicates a bearish corrective wave.

True   False

13. An exponential moving average (EMA) gives more weight to recent data and doesn't abruptly drop old data.

True   False

14. The MACD line is the difference between a fast EMA and a slower EMA.

True   False

15. The signal line is an EMA of the MACD line.

    True   False

16. The MACD histogram is the difference between the fast EMA and the signal line.

    True   False

17. When the MACD histogram crosses from below zero to above zero, it means that the fast EMA has crossed above the slow EMA.

    True   False

18. Today's directional movement can be defined as the largest part of today's range that is outside yesterday's range.

    True   False

19. If the DMI spread is above zero, we know that a stock is in a strong uptrend.

    True   False

20. In an uptrend, the parabolic indicator's dots rise after days that make new highs for the trade but stay the same after days that don't make new highs.

    True   False

21. Ratios generated by the Fibonacci number series were known and applied in many fields (e.g., art, architecture, and music) centuries before Fibonacci wrote about the series in the 1200s.

    True   False

22. Many traders look for 38.2% and 61.8% retracements of impulse waves; alternatively, traders can look for retracements within a Fibonacci retracement zone extending from 38.2% to 61.8% of impulse waves.

     True   False

Note. The following questions refer specifically to the *First Prize* strategy:

23. The *First Prize* strategy buys after a rally in a downtrend and sells short after a decline in an uptrend.

     True   False

24. The trend is up if EMA:13 is greater than EMA:34.

     True   False

25. A new 21-day high is required as part of the strategy's buy setup.

     True   False

26. In a buy setup, the DMI spread must remain above +15 at least until the entry occurs.

     True   False

27. In a setup to sell short, the close must be either a 38.2% or a 61.8% retracement of the impulse wave.

     True   False

28. In a buy setup, the MACD line must cross below the signal line for the first time since the signal line crossed above zero.

     True   False

29. In a setup to sell short, the MACD histogram can be either rising or falling on the day before a sell order is placed.

True   False

30. When a buy setup is in effect, go long on the next day's open.

True   False

31. After selling a stock short, place an initial protective stop above the high of the corrective wave.

True   False

32. It's unfortunate, but the *First Prize* strategy can be applied only to stocks and can be traded only on the daily time frame.

True   False

Chapter 5

R2D2

Prices move in trends and trends tend to continue until
something happens to change the supply-demand balance.
Such changes are usually detectable in the action of the
market itself. Certain patterns or formations, levels or areas,
appear on the charts which have a meaning and can be
interpreted in terms of probable future trend development.
They are not infallible, it must be noted, but the odds are
definitely in their favor. Time after time, as experience has
amply proved, they are far more prescient than the best
informed and most shrewd of statisticians.
—Robert D. Edwards and John Magee, *Technical*
Analysis of Stock Trends (John Magee Inc.,
Springfield, Massachusetts, 1948)

My *R2D2* strategy is based on a pattern called *reverse divergence* that very accurately forecasts the resumption of strong trends after corrective waves. I named the strategy after R2D2, the unimpressive-looking but efficient and resourceful little droid in the *Star Wars* movies. *R2D2* seemed a suitable name for the strategy I'd been abbreviating *RD* for *reverse divergence*. Before tackling reverse divergence and the *R2D2* strategy, let's consider the term *divergence*. One of its uses in technical analysis is to describe the situation in which prices make a new high or low but a momentum oscillator (an indicator that measures the acceleration or deceleration of price changes) fails to make a new high or low. The new price high or low is not confirmed by a similar pattern in the oscillator. A bearish-divergence top indicates that bullish momentum was weaker at the current high than it was at the previous high; a bullish-divergence bottom means that bearish momentum was weaker on the current low than on the previous low (see Figure 5.1).

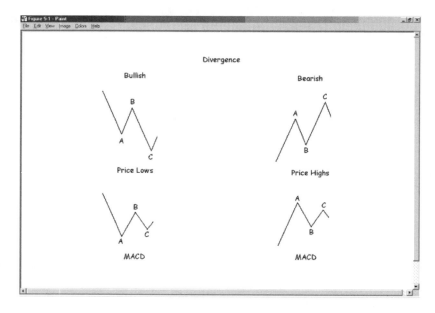

Figure 5.1   Normal bullish and bearish divergences.

In a bullish divergence, the price low at C is below the price low at A, while the MACD at C is above the MACD at A. In a bearish divergence, the price high at C is above the price high at B, while the MACD at C is below the MACD at A.

Reverse divergences, on the other hand, are formed when a momentum oscillator makes a new high or low but prices fail to make a new high or low. A bullish reverse divergence occurs when prices hold above the previous low but an oscillator declines to a lower low; a bearish reverse divergence is formed when prices hover below the previous high but an oscillator rises to a new high (see Figures 5.2 and 5.3).

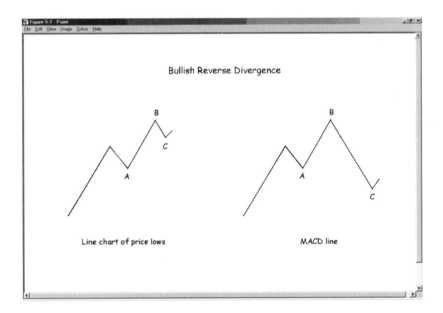

Figure 5.2   The price low at C is above the price low at A, while the MACD at C is below the MACD at A.

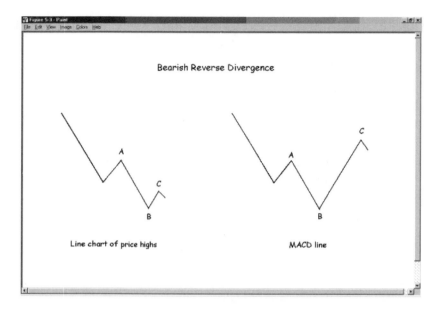

Figure 5.3   The price high at C is below the price high at A, while the MACD at C is above the MACD at A.

A bullish reverse divergence is like a jump ball in basketball: Before the referee tosses the ball up, the two players bend their legs and crouch low so that they can leap higher when the ball is in the air. A bearish reverse divergence is like the Twilight Zone Tower of Terror attraction at Disney World. First, an elevator takes riders part way up the tower and drops them for a fairly unsettling few seconds; then, the elevator rises again—higher than the first time—and drops the riders for a faster and longer descent. The elevator's second ascent is like an oscillator climbing higher than it did on its previous ascent: After a bearish reverse divergence, prices often fall farther and more quickly than they did on their previous decline.

In the stock and futures markets, reverse divergences frequently lead to substantial price swings in the direction of a market's underlying trend. Following are the rules for *R2D2*, my reverse-divergence strategy.

R2D2: The Rules

To trade the *R2D2* strategy, you'll need the following technical tools: a Japanese candlestick chart (or a bar chart), a 55-day EMA, a 13-day DMI spread, and a 3-8-13-day MACD. The setup, entry, and exits for *R2D2* follow.

Trading the Long Side

Setup

1. Closing prices are above the EMA throughout the setup.

2. The MACD line forms a bullish reverse divergence.

3. The DMI spread is greater than +15 at point B (refer to Figure 5.4 on page 104).

4. The MACD histogram is higher than it was yesterday.

5. Although not required, candlestick patterns appear frequently in *R2D2* setups and provide additional confirmation for a trade.

Entry

Buy today above yesterday's high.

Exits

1. Set an initial protective stop below the higher of the two lows of the reverse-divergence pattern (refer to Figure 5.4, point C) or below the low of the entry day, whichever is lower.

2. After a close above the highest high between the two lows of the reverse-divergence pattern (refer to Figure 5.4, point B), raise the protective stop to breakeven and trail a tight stop to lock in most of the open profits while still giving the market some room to run.

Trading the Short Side

Setup

1. Closing prices are below the EMA throughout the setup.

2. The MACD line forms a bearish reverse divergence.

3. The DMI spread is less than −15 at point B (refer to Figure 5.9 on page 110).

4. The MACD histogram is lower than it was yesterday.

5. Although not required, candlestick patterns appear frequently in *R2D2* setups and provide additional confirmation for a trade.

Entry

Sell short today below yesterday's low.

Exits

1. Set an initial protective stop above the lower of the two highs of the reverse-divergence pattern (refer to Figure 5.9, point C) or above the high of the entry day, whichever is higher.

2. After a close below the lowest low between the two highs of the reverse-divergence pattern (refer to Figure 5.9, point B), lower the protective stop to breakeven and trail a tight protective stop to lock in most of the open profits while still giving the market some room to run.

Before we look at our examples of *R2D2* trades, I'd like to make two points. First, since the setups for all the trades are identical—they all fulfill the conditions for reverse-divergence setups explained above—I'll review the setup conditions here but won't reiterate the setup conditions in the commentary for each trade. Here are the *R2D2* setup conditions: For a long trade, closing prices stay above the moving average throughout the setup, the MACD line completes a bullish reverse divergence at point C, and the DMI spread rises above +15 at point B; for a short trade, closing prices stay below the moving average throughout the setup, the MACD line completes a bearish reverse divergence at point C, and the DMI spread falls below −15 at point B.

My second point is a reminder about exit techniques: For each trade, I selected an exit that let profits run but that didn't give back too much of the open profits. Some other exit techniques would have worked even better, and others would not have worked as well. As you study the exits I've used in these examples, please keep in mind that you should strive to become an expert in just a few of the exit techniques and stick with them in your own trading.

Figure 5.4 is a daily chart of Albertsons (ABS). Note that prices form a small symmetrical triangle (not uncommon in an *R2D2* setup), providing additional confirmation for the trade. After a bullish reverse-divergence setup, the MACD histogram turns up at C, so we buy on the next day above the high of candle C, and we set an initial protective stop below the low of C. Three days after C, ABS closes above the high of the reverse-divergence pattern (point B), so we raise the protective stop to

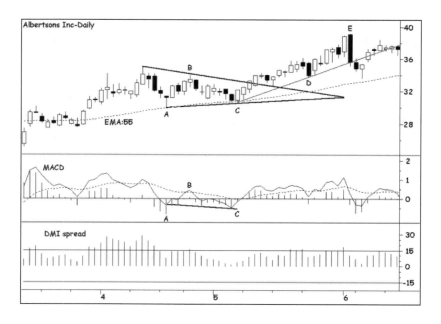

Figure 5.4   Albertsons Inc.

breakeven (our entry price). Let's use a trendline to signal our exit from this trade. Two days after candle D (when we know that D has become a swing low with a strength of two), we draw a trendline connecting the swing lows at C and D and trail our stop just below the trendline. The bearish engulfing line at E penetrates the trendline and triggers our stop, closing out the trade.

Figure 5.5 is a daily chart of the Apollo Group (APOL). Note that candle C is a hammer, and the next candle is a bullish engulfing line, so prospects look good for an upswing in prices. The MACD histogram turns up on the day after C, and we buy APOL on the next day above the day C high. Next, we set our initial protective stop

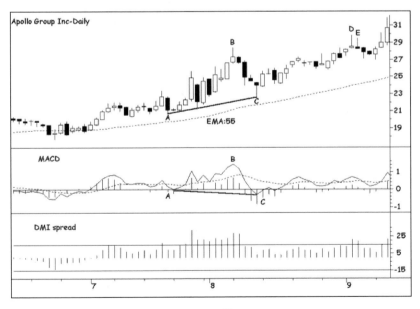

Figure 5.5 Apollo Group Inc.

below the low of C and wait for APOL to close above point B, the high of the reverse-divergence pattern. Candle D closes above the point B high, so we move our stop to breakeven. For this trade, let's trail a stop at the two-day low. Candles D and E are both shooting stars—a bearish pattern—and the candle after E falls below the lows at D and E, stopping us out of the trade.

Figure 5.6 is a daily chart of the Atmel Corporation (ATML), with a reverse-divergence setup culminating the day after candle C with a bullish engulfing line that pulled the MACD histogram higher. We buy on the second candle after C, above the previous day's high, and set our initial protective stop below the point C low. At D, ATML closes above the point B high, so we raise our

Figure 5.6   Atmel Corp.

106

stop to breakeven. Let's exit this trade on candle E, below a trendline drawn from the swing low three days after D to the swing low six days later.

Figure 5.7 is a daily chart of Bea Systems (BEAS). Candle C, a bullish engulfing line, pulls the MACD histogram up, so we buy on the next day when BEAS gaps open above the candle C high, creating a bullish window (gap). Our entry day turns out to be a doji (implying a stalemate between the bulls and bears), the second candle after C closes the window (fills the gap), and the third candle after C is another doji. Although the candles immediately following our entry aren't particularly encouraging, our initial protective stop below the low of candle C isn't threatened, and the trade gets back on track four

Figure 5.7   Bea Systems.

days after C, posting the highest closing price since our entry. Candle D closes above the high at point B, so we raise our stop to breakeven. For this trade, let's employ our basic two-day trailing stop, exiting on candle E (which turns out to be a bearish engulfing line) when prices fall below the two-day low.

Figure 5.8 is a daily chart of the EMC Corporation (EMC), featuring two bullish reverse-divergence trades. In the first, the MACD histogram turns up on the day after C, so we buy on the next day (candle D), which gaps higher, creating a bullish window, and we set our

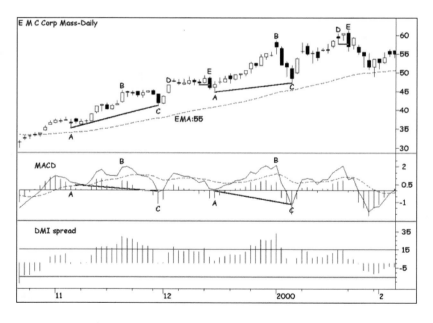

Figure 5.8 EMC Corporation.

initial protective stop below the low of candle C. Candle D closes above the high of candle B, so we raise our protective stop from the low at C to breakeven. Let's stick with the two-day trailing stop, exiting the trade at point E, which makes a new two-day low and becomes a bearish engulfing line. The setup for the second EMC trade on this chart begins the day after we exit the first trade. The MACD histogram turns up on the day after C, so we buy on the next day's higher open and set our initial protective stop below the candle C low. Our entry candle becomes a *gravestone doji*—a candle that opens and closes at the same (or nearly the same) price, with its small real body near the bottom of a long upper shadow. Our entry day is followed by a bearish engulfing line, a harami cross, another bearish engulfing line, and finally, two more dojis. This six-day sequence is not encouraging, but, nevertheless, the candle before D closes above the high at B, so we raise the protective stop to breakeven. For this trade, a two-day trailing stop provides a timely exit (with a small gain on the trade) at candle E, when the stock falls to a new two-day low.

Figure 5.9, a daily chart of Aon Corporation (AOC), shows an *R2D2* trade from the short side. The candle at C is a harami cross, suggesting that the countertrend rally might be weakening, and the MACD histogram turns down the next day. We sell short two days after C, below the previous day's low, and we set our initial protective stop above the high of candle C. Candle D closes below the low of candle B, so we lower the stop to breakeven. For this trade, let's apply a parabolic trailing stop to lock

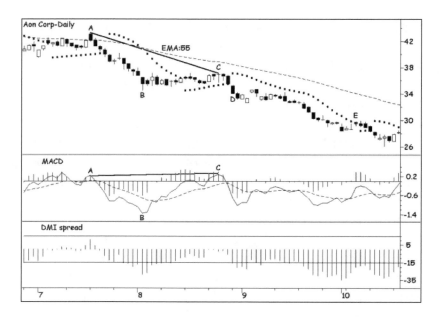

Figure 5.9   Aon Corporation.

in an increasing amount of open profit until we're eventually stopped out of the trade at E.

Figure 5.10 is a daily chart of Ensco International (ESV). Candle C, a bearish engulfing line, pushes the MACD histogram down, so we sell short on the next day below the candle C low. We set our initial protective stop above the high of the candle after C (because it's higher than the candle C high). Next, we lower the stop to breakeven after candle D, which closes below the low at point B. For this trade, let's use the DMI spread as an exit technique: When the spread crosses from below zero to above zero, we'll exit on the next day's open. At point E, the amount of upward directional movement exceeds

110

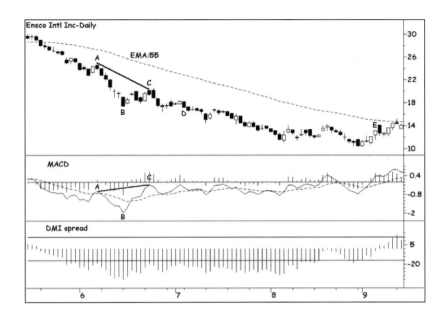

Figure 5.10   Ensco International.

the amount of downward directional movement (the DMI spread crosses above zero) for the first time since our entry into this trade, so it may be a propitious time to take our profits in ESV and look for a promising setup in another stock.

Figure 5.11 is a daily chart of Fifth Third Bancorp (FITB). The MACD histogram turns down on the candle after C (a harami), so we sell short two days after C below the previous day's low and set our initial protective stop above the candle C high. Candle D closes below the low at B, so we lower the stop to breakeven. Let's exit this trade on candle E, when prices rally above the two-day high.

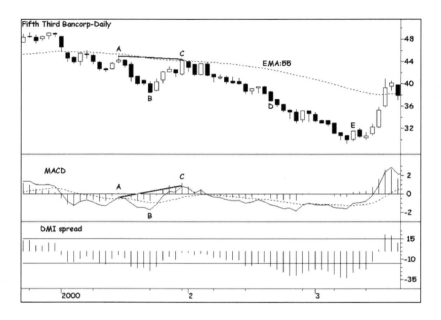

Figure 5.11 Fifth Third Bancorp.

Figure 5.12 is a daily chart of Linens N Things (LIN). The MACD histogram turns down on the day after C, so we sell short two days after C below the previous day's low and set our initial protective stop above the high of candle C. Candle D closes below the low of candle B, so we lower the stop to breakeven. For this trade, let's exit with the MACD indicator: After the MACD line crosses above the signal line at E, we take our profits on the next day's open.

Figure 5.13 is a daily chart of the NASDAQ 100 Trust (QQQ). The bearish reverse-divergence pattern is followed by a harami cross and a bearish engulfing line.

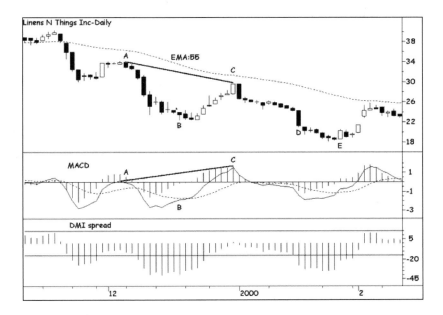

Figure 5.12   Linens N Things.

The MACD histogram turns down on the day of the harami cross, and we sell short the next day below the low of the harami cross. We set our initial protective stop above the high of candle C and lower the stop to breakeven after candle D, which closes below the low of candle B. For this trade, let's exit when prices penetrate the bearish trendline drawn from the swing high four days before D to the swing high three days after D. The trendline is confirmed (it gets a third touch) at the swing high 10 days after D, and we exit on candle E when prices break above the trendline. Note the two doji

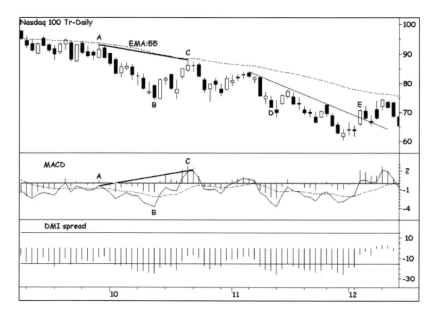

Figure 5.13   NASDAQ 100 Trust (QQQ).

candles before candle E and the small window (in this case, a bullish breakaway gap) between the second doji and candle E, which confirms our decision to exit at this point.

Figure 5.14 is a weekly chart of Macrovision (MVSN). The MACD histogram turns up on the candle after C, and we buy on the next candle above the previous candle's high. We set our initial protective stop below the low of candle C and raise the stop to breakeven after candle D, which closes above the high of candle B. For this trade, let's use the MACD indicator as our exit technique:

114

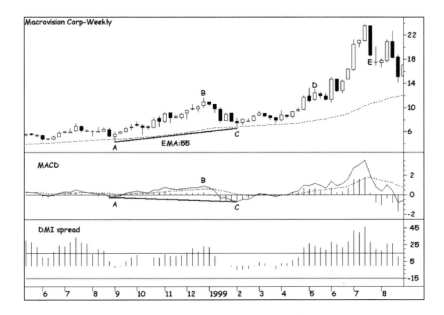

Figure 5.14 Macrovision.

The MACD line crosses below the signal line at point E, so we sell on the next candle's open.

Figure 5.15, a weekly chart of Maxim (MXIM), shows two *R2D2* trades. In the first setup, the MACD histogram turns up at C, so we buy on the candle after C above the previous candle's high, and we set our initial protective stop below the low of candle C. Candle D closes above the high of candle B, so we raise the stop to breakeven. The second setup on this chart is completed on candle C2, a doji, which suggests that the brief countertrend decline may be over (the next two candles are

115

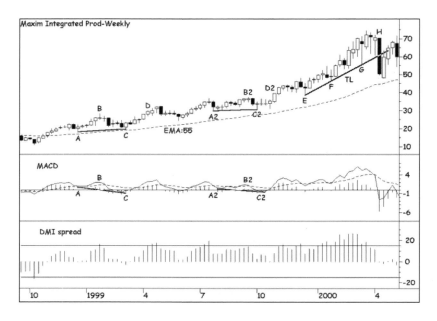

Figure 5.15 Maxim.

also dojis). The candle after C2 pulls the MACD histogram up, and we enter a new long position on the fourth candle after C2, above the previous candle's high. We set our initial protective stop below the low of candle C2 and raise the stop to breakeven after candle D2. Let's exit both trades on candle H when prices penetrate the trendline connecting swing lows E, F, and G.

Figure 5.16 is a weekly chart of Adelphia Communications (ADLAC). Candle C pushes the MACD histogram down, so we sell short on the next candle below the low of candle C. We set our initial protective stop above the

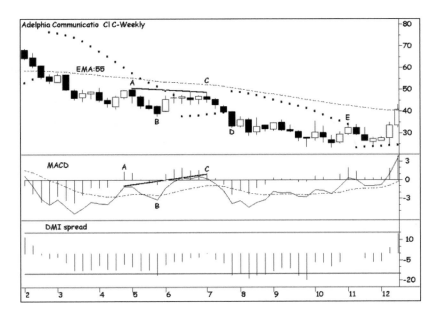

Figure 5.16 Adelphia Communications.

high of the candle two weeks before C (the high of the reverse-divergence pattern). Next, we lower the stop to breakeven after candle D, which closes below the low of candle B. For this trade, the parabolic indicator provides an efficient exit on candle E.

Figure 5.17 is a weekly chart of Standard & Poor's Depository Receipts, (SPDRs) for short (symbol SPY). SPY trades like a single stock, but it provides ownership in the 500 stocks that make up the S&P 500 Index. The MACD histogram turns down at C, which is both a shooting star and a harami, and we sell short on the next candle below

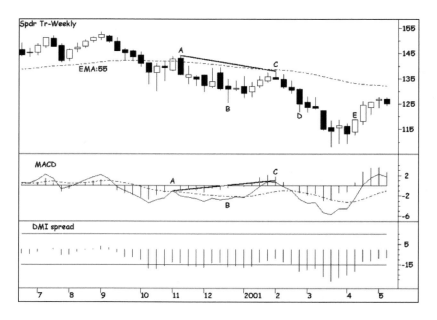

Figure 5.17 Standard & Poor's Depository
Receipts (SPDRs).

the low of candle C. We set our initial protective stop
above the high of candle C and lower the stop to
breakeven after candle D, which closes below the low of
candle B. For this trade, let's use a two-week trailing
stop, exiting on candle E when prices exceed the highs of
the previous two candles.

Figure 5.18 is a two-minute chart of IBM. The MACD
histogram turns up on the candle after C, so we buy on
candle D above the high of C and set our initial protective
stop below the low of candle C (on a two-minute chart,

118

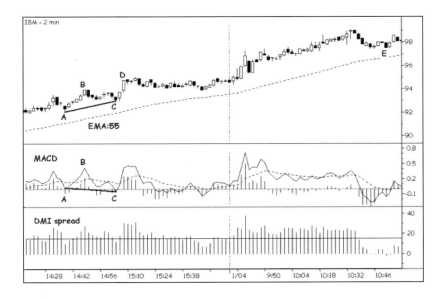

Figure 5.18 IBM.

we'll keep a *mental* stop rather than placing and replacing stops in such a short time frame; we'll exit at the market (that is, at the best price available at that moment) if prices fall to the low of candle C). After candle D, which closes above the high at B, we raise our mental stop to breakeven. Let's use the DMI spread indicator as our signal to exit this trade: The DMI spread crosses from above zero to below zero on candle E, so we take our profits on the next candle.

Figure 5.19 is a three-minute chart of JDS Uniphase (JDSU). Candle C and the candle before C are dojis, so

119

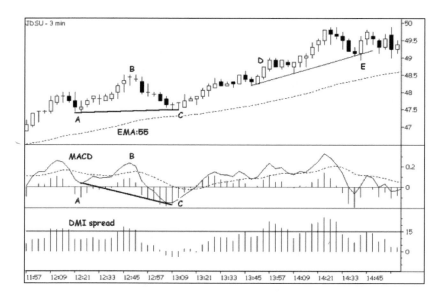

Figure 5.19 JDS Uniphase.

the countertrend decline may be near its end. The MACD histogram turns up on the candle before C, so we buy on candle C above the previous candle's high and set our mental stop below the low of candle C. Candle D closes above the high of candle B, so we raise our mental stop to breakeven. Let's exit this trade on candle E when prices fall below the bullish trendline.

Figure 5.20 is a 10-minute chart of Nortel Networks (NT). The candle after candle C is a harami cross, which implies that the countertrend decline may be losing steam, and the MACD histogram turns up on the second

120

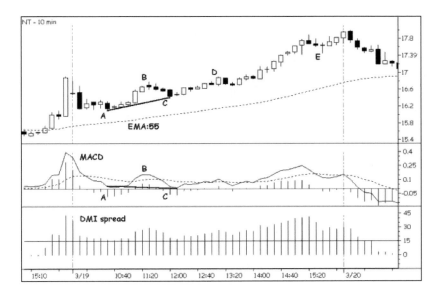

Figure 5.20 Nortel Networks.

candle after C. We buy on the next candle above the previous candle's high and set our initial protective stop below the low of candle C (on a 10-minute chart, it's not unreasonable to actually place the stop in the market, but you can keep a mental stop if you prefer). Candle D closes above the high of candle B, so we raise the stop to breakeven. Let's exit the trade at point E when prices make a new two-period low.

Figure 5.21 is a 15-minute chart of Dell Computer (DELL). The MACD histogram turns down on the candle after C, so we sell short on the next candle below the

121

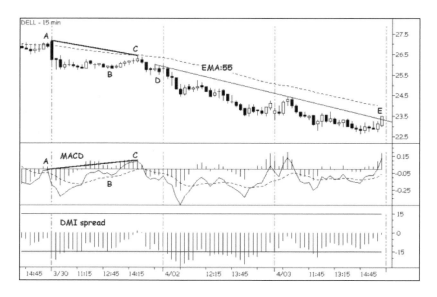

Figure 5.21 Dell Computer.

previous candle's low and set our initial protective stop above the high of candle C. Candle D closes below the low of candle B, so we lower the stop to breakeven. Let's exit the trade on candle E when prices penetrate the bearish trendline.

Figure 5.22 is a 10-minute chart of the EMC Corporation (EMC). The MACD histogram turns down on the doji candle after C. We sell short on the second candle after C below the previous candle's low and set our initial protective stop above the high of C. Candle D closes below the low of candle B, so we lower the stop to breakeven. Let's apply a measured-move exit strategy to

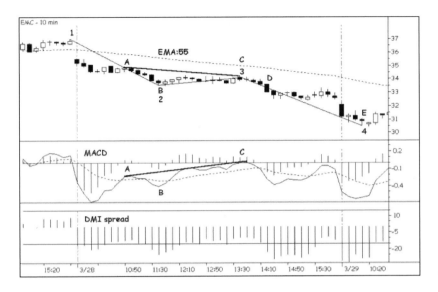

Figure 5.22 EMC Corporation.

this trade. When the distance from the swing high at point 1 to the swing low at point 2 is equaled by the downward move from point 3 (the high of the reverse-divergence pattern), we'll exit the trade. The price swing from point 1 to point 2 is replicated by the price swing from point 3 to point 4, so we cover our short position on candle E.

Next, let's study some *R2D2* trades in the futures markets. Figure 5.23 shows two consecutive long trades on a daily chart of crude oil (CL). The first candle C is a doji that marks the end of the countertrend decline. The candle after C pulls the MACD histogram higher, so we buy on the next day when prices gap open above the previous

123

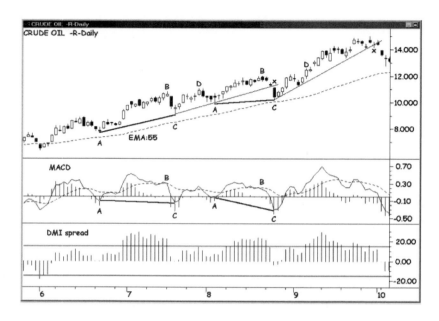

Figure 5.23 Crude oil.

day's high. We set our initial protective stop below the low of candle C and raise the stop to breakeven after candle D, which closes above the high at B. Let's exit the trade at the first point X, when prices open below the trendline that connects the low at point C of the first setup to the low at point A of the second setup. The setup for the second trade on this chart is completed with a harami pattern on the candle after C that also pulls the MACD histogram higher. We enter a new long position on the next day above the high of the harami and set our initial protective stop below the low of candle C. We raise

124

the stop to breakeven after candle D, which closes above the high at B. Let's exit this trade at the second point X, when prices fall below the trendline drawn from the swing low at C to the swing low two days before D.

Figure 5.24 is a daily chart of Dow Jones futures (DJ). The candle after C pulls the MACD histogram higher, but we don't buy on the next day (a harami) because prices don't penetrate the previous day's high. We enter a new long position three days after C above the harami's high and set our initial protective stop below the low of candle

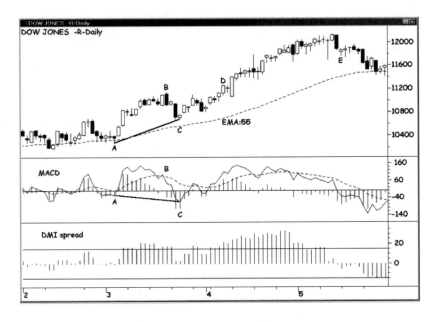

Figure 5.24 Dow futures.

C. Candle D closes above the high of candle B, so we raise the stop to breakeven. Let's take our profits on this trade at the open of candle E, the day after the DMI spread crosses from above zero to below zero.

Figure 5.25 shows two consecutive *R2D2* short trades on a daily chart of Canadian dollar futures (CD). The first setup is completed at point C, a bearish engulfing line that pushes the MACD histogram down. The candle after C is a harami, so we don't sell short until the next day, when prices fall below the previous day's low. We set our initial protective stop above the high of candle C and lower the stop to breakeven after candle D, which closes below the low at B. The second setup is completed at the

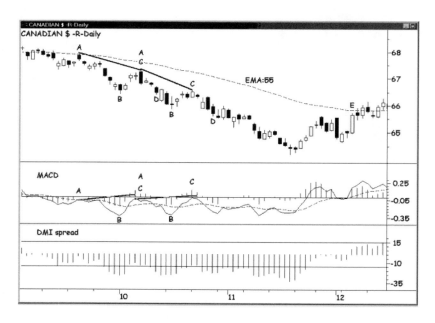

Figure 5.25   Canadian dollar.

126

second point C (which I'll refer to as C2), and the next day's harami pushes the MACD histogram down. We sell short again on the day after the harami below the harami's low and set our initial protective stop above the high of candle C2. Candle D2 closes below the low of the candle at B2, so we lower the stop to breakeven. Let's cover both short positions on the next open after the DMI spread crosses from below zero to above zero at E.

Figure 5.26 is a daily chart of Japanese yen futures. Candle C is a doji pattern, which suggests that the countertrend rally might be near its demise. Candle C pushes the MACD histogram lower, so we sell short on the next candle's lower open and set our initial protective stop

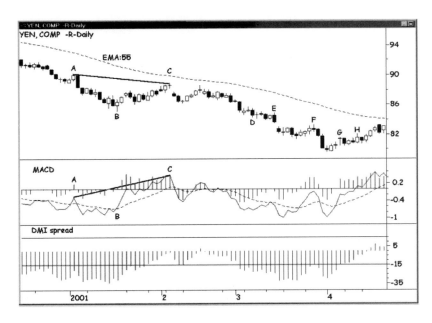

Figure 5.26 Japanese yen.

above the high of candle C. After candle D closes below the low of candle B, we lower the stop to breakeven. To exit this trade, let's trail a stop at the previous swing high (with a strength of two or greater). Swing highs E, F, and G become our trailing stops, and we are eventually stopped out of this trade with a considerable profit at H when prices rally above the swing high at G.

Figure 5.27 is a weekly chart of crude oil futures (CL). The candle after C pulls the MACD histogram higher. We buy on the candle two weeks after C, above the previous week's high. We set our initial protective stop below the low of candle C and raise the stop to breakeven after candle D, which closes above the high of candle B. For this

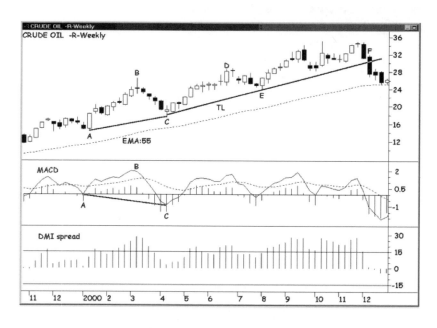

Figure 5.27 Crude oil.

trade, let's trail a stop below the trendline drawn from the swing low at point C to the swing low at point E. An evening star pattern—a bearish sign—forms during the three weeks before F, and we take our profits at F when prices fall below the trendline.

Figure 5.28 is a weekly chart of Nikkei Index futures (NK). The MACD histogram turns down on the candle after C, so we sell short on the second candle after C, which gaps lower on the open. We set our initial protective stop above the high of candle C and lower the stop to breakeven after candle D closes below the low of candle B. For this trade, let's use the parabolic indicator to lock in profits as the trade matures and to generate a timely exit signal on candle E.

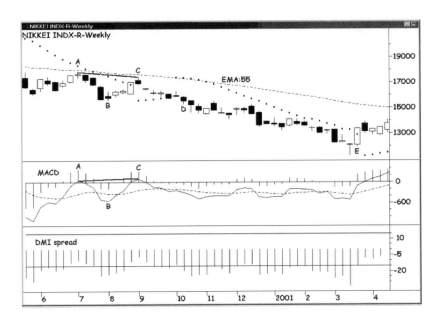

Figure 5.28 Nikkei Index.

Summary

In 1991, I made my first major presentation about technical analysis and trading at the thirteenth annual Technical Analysis Group (TAG) conference in Washington, D.C. The first question in the question-and-answer session was this: "In an uptrend, if an oscillator makes a lower low, but a market makes a higher low, is that bullish or bearish?" I replied, "I haven't really done any research on that, but since we use oscillators—like MACD, RSI, or stochastics—to give us added insight into a market's price behavior, I'd have to say that a market will usually do what the oscillator says it should do. In the example you gave, the market will usually follow the oscillator and fall to a lower low in the very near future." Boy, was I wrong! The pattern the questioner described was, of course, reverse divergence. My *R2D2* strategy adds more technical indicators, candlestick patterns, and a variety of stops to take full advantage of the powerful reverse-divergence pattern.

The next strategy we'll study, *Triple Play*, completes the *Playing for Keeps* arsenal of trading strategies that consistently beat the markets. *First Prize* trades first pullbacks, *R2D2* trades subsequent pullbacks, and *Triple Play* trades trend reversals, buying low and selling high.

Chapter 5 Quiz

1. In a normal bullish divergence, a stock makes a low, rallies, and then falls to a lower low, whereas a momentum oscillator makes a low along with prices, rallies, and then puts in a higher low.

   True   False

2. In a bullish reverse divergence, a stock makes a low, rallies, and then puts in a higher low, whereas a momentum oscillator makes a low along with prices, rallies, and then falls to a lower low.

   True   False

3. Normal divergences usually occur in the direction of the trend they are following, whereas reverse divergences usually occur against that trend.

   True   False

Note: The following questions refer specifically to the *R2D2* strategy:

4. For a bullish setup to remain in effect, closing prices must remain above the 55-day EMA throughout the entire setup.

   True   False

5. For a bearish setup, the MACD line may form either a normal divergence or a reverse divergence.

   True   False

6. An order to sell short should be placed only if today's MACD histogram is less than it was yesterday.

True   False

7. If a bullish setup is in effect, place an order to buy above yesterday's high.

True   False

Chapter 6

TRIPLE PLAY

The various formations and patterns we have studied are not meaningless or arbitrary. They signify changes in real values; the expectations, hopes, fears, developments in the industry; and all other factors that are known to anyone. It is not necessary that we know, in each case, what particular hopes, fears, or developments are represented by a certain pattern. It is important that we recognize that pattern and understand what results may be expected to emerge from it.
—Robert D. Edwards and John Magee, *Technical Analysis of Stock Trends* (John Magee Inc., Springfield, Massachusetts, 1948)

My *Triple Play* strategy is based on divergence patterns between the MACD and prices when a market completes a series of rallies to three or more higher highs or three or more declines to lower lows. The premise behind the strategy is that changes in the trend of *momentum* precede changes in the trend of *prices;* therefore, MACD's

135

failure to confirm new price highs and lows is a compelling early warning sign that a change in trend may be imminent. In *Triple Play*, we'll rely on an exponential moving average (EMA) channel as our trend indicator and the MACD as our momentum indicator. (Some technicians consider the MACD to be more of a trend-following indicator than a momentum indicator because it is based on moving averages and has no fixed upper and lower boundaries as momentum indicators like the relative strength index and stochastics do. However, since the MACD line measures the acceleration or deceleration of the spread between two moving averages, thus measuring the acceleration or deceleration of a fast moving average toward or away from a slow moving average, I consider it more of a momentum indicator than a trend-following one). To see what bullish multiple divergences look like, let's turn to Figure 6.1.

Let's consider Figure 6.1 first. In the type 1 bullish divergence pattern, both prices and the MACD fall to a new low for the current downtrend. Then, after a countertrend rally, prices make a second new low, but the MACD does not fall below its previous low. Finally, after a second rally, prices make a third new low, but the MACD posts its highest low of the series. In short, the MACD makes a low along with prices and then posts two higher lows while prices post two lower lows.

The type 2 bullish divergence pattern starts out the same as type 1, as both prices and the MACD fall to new lows for the current downswing, and the MACD fails to make a second new low along with prices. In this type of divergence pattern, however, when prices make a third new low, the MACD's third decline bottoms out *between*

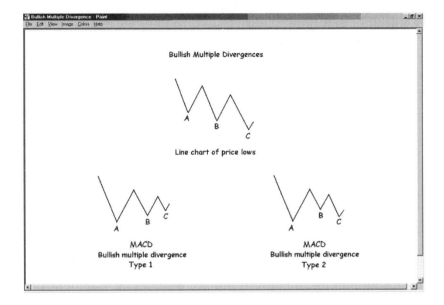

Figure 6.1   The line chart of price lows indicates lower lows at B and C, the type 1 divergence indicates higher lows at B and C, and the type 2 divergence indicates a higher low at B but a low between A and B at C.

its first and second lows. In other words, the third MACD low is higher than its first low but lower than its second one.

Next, let's consider the bearish multiple divergences in Figure 6.2. In the type 1 bearish divergence pattern, both prices and the MACD rise to a new high for the current uptrend. Then, after a countertrend decline, prices make a second new high, but the MACD does not exceed its previous high. Finally, after a second decline, prices make a third new high, but the MACD posts its lowest high of the series. In short, the MACD makes a high

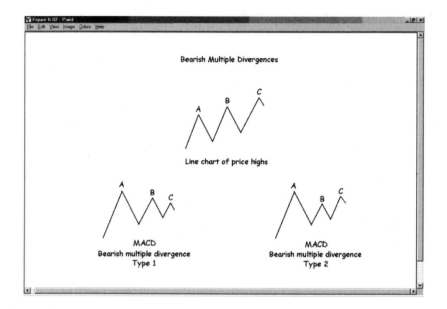

Figure 6.2 The line chart of price highs shows higher highs at B and C, the type 1 divergence shows lower MACD highs at B and C, and the type 2 divergence shows a lower MACD high at B but an MACD high at C between the highs at A and B.

along with prices and then posts two lower highs while prices post two higher highs.

The type 2 bearish divergence pattern starts out the same as type 1, as both prices and the MACD rise to new highs for the current uptrend, and the MACD fails to make a second new high along with prices. In this type of divergence pattern, however, when prices make a third new high, the MACD's third rally tops out *between* its first and second highs. In other words, the third MACD high is lower than its first high but higher than its second one.

With that understanding of the multiple divergence patterns between prices and the MACD, we can turn our attention to the strategy's rules for setups, entries, and exits.

Triple Play: The Rules

To trade my *Triple Play* strategy, you'll need the following technical tools: a Japanese candlestick chart (or a bar chart), an exponential moving-average (EMA) channel of 13 highs and 13 lows, and a 3-8-13 MACD. The setup, entry, and exits for *Triple Play* follow.

Trading the Long Side

Setup
1. The lows of the three (or more) declines that comprise the multiple divergence pattern must all be below the EMA channel.
2. The MACD line must form a multiple bullish divergence pattern.

Entry
1. Buy when prices penetrate the top of the EMA channel (the basic entry technique).
2. In addition to the basic entry technique, consider other factors, such as breakaway gaps, candlestick

patterns, and trendlines, to fine-tune your entry. These tools often provide an earlier entry (and a better entry price) without eroding the accuracy of the strategy.

Exits

1. Set an initial protective stop below the low of candle C (the low of the multiple divergence pattern).
2. Trail a stop to lock in some profits while giving the market some room to run.

Trading the Short Side

Setup

1. The highs of the three (or more) rallies that comprise the multiple divergence pattern must all be above the EMA channel.
2. The MACD line must form a multiple bearish divergence pattern.

Entry

1. Sell short when prices penetrate the bottom of the EMA channel (the basic entry technique).
2. In addition to the basic entry technique, consider other factors, such as breakaway gaps, candlestick patterns, and trendlines, to fine-tune your entry. These tools often provide an earlier entry (and a better entry price) without eroding the accuracy of the strategy.

Exits

1. Set an initial protective stop above the high of candle C (the high of the multiple divergence pattern).
2. Trail a stop to lock in some profits while giving the market some room to run.

Before we begin our study of *Triple Play* examples, let me make two points: First, the setups for all the trades are multiple consecutive divergences, and the initial protective stops are all below the low of candle C for a long position and above the high of candle C for a short position, so I won't reiterate the setups or initial protective stops in the commentary for each trade. Second, for each example, I selected an exit technique that I thought was not only effective but also educational. As you study the exits in the *Triple Play* trades, please take time to see how your favorite exit techniques would have fared in these examples. Ideally, the exit techniques that you will employ in your own trading should (a) limit your initial risk, (b) give your trade some time to develop in the expected direction, (c) lock in some of your open profits, and (d) let you exit quickly when the trend appears to have run its course. That's asking a lot, but the markets wouldn't pay us so generously for being good traders if it were easy.

Figure 6.3 is a daily chart of Agilent Technologies (AGIL). Note the morning star candlestick pattern that's completed at D. There are three reasonable ways to enter this trade: (1) buy on the candle after D when prices exceed candle D's high, (2) buy on candle E when prices break the bearish trendline, and (3) buy on candle E

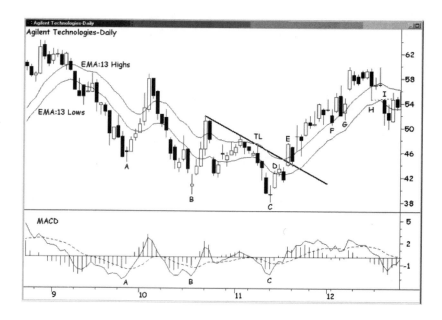

Figure 6.3　Agilent Technologies.

when prices penetrate the top of the EMA channel. Here are three ways to trail a stop and to exit this trade: (1) trail a stop below the EMA channel; (2) raise the stop to below the swing lows (strength of two or greater) at F, G, and H—exiting on candle I; or (3) exit at the parabolic stop (shown in Figure 6.4).

Figure 6.5 is a daily chart of Forest Labs (FRX). On the candle after C, we know that candle C is a swing low and that a tweezer top is in place. Buying on candle D when it gaps open above the tweezer top is aggressive, but not

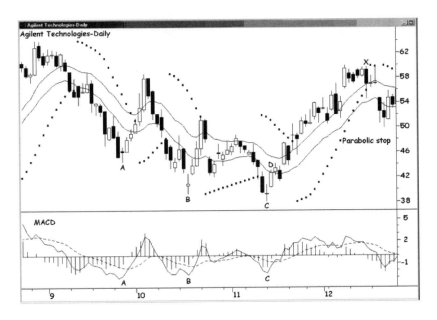

Figure 6.4   Agilent technologies with parabolic exit.

unreasonable; buying when candle D penetrates the top of the EMA channel is a bit more conservative. Trail a stop below the channel or below the swing lows (strength of two or greater) at E, F, and G. Note the *measuring gap* (window) between the second and third candles after F (a measuring gap frequently marks the halfway point of a trend), the *exhaustion gap* between the first and second candles after G (an exhaustion gap warns of a possible trend reversal), and the *breakaway gap* between candles H and I (a breakaway gap often

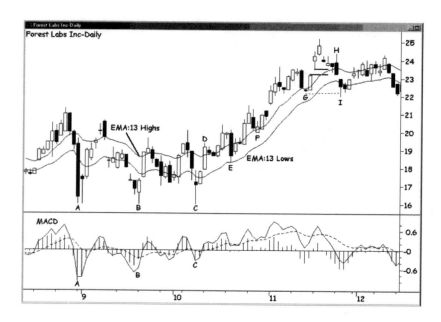

Figure 6.5   Forest Labs.

begins a new trend in the opposite direction of the current trend). The exhaustion gap and the breakaway gap form an *island reversal:* The six candles between the gaps are like an island—there's "open water" to the left and right. There are at least four reasonable ways to exit this trade: (1) exit on candle I's gap-lower open (because it creates an island reversal), (2) exit when candle I falls below the EMA channel, (3) exit when candle I falls below the swing low at G, or (4) exit at the parabolic stop on the candle marked with an X on Figure 6.6.

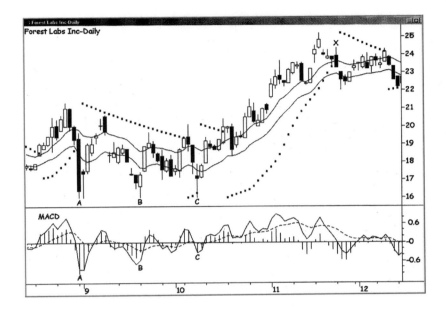

Figure 6.6   Forest labs with parabolic exit.

Figure 6.7 is a daily chart of Biogen (BGEN), showing a bearish multiple divergence pattern. Candle D, a harami, and candle E, a bearish engulfing line, suggest that the uptrend may be languishing; candle E's decline below the bullish trendline and the EMA channel confirm the change in trend. Trail a stop above the channel or above the swing highs at F, G, H, and I. Because candle J is a piercing line (a strong bullish pattern), it would be prudent to lower the stop to just above its high and to exit on the next candle.

145

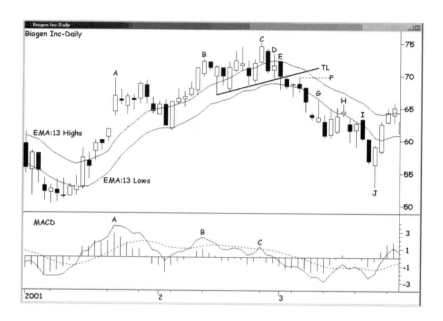

Figure 6.7 Biogen.

Figure 6.8 is a daily chart of Computer Associates (CA). The candle after C is a harami, and candle D breaks the bullish trendline. Sell short on the trendline break or the penetration of the EMA channel on the candle after D. Trail a stop above the channel or above the swing highs at E, F, G, and I. Candle H is a hammer, a bullish warning. Exit on candle J when it exceeds the swing high at I or the top of the channel. Figure 6.9 shows an even more timely exit at the parabolic stop (marked X).

Figure 6.10 is a weekly chart of Seagram (VO). Candle D completes a pattern that's almost a morning star (there's no window between the first and second can-

146

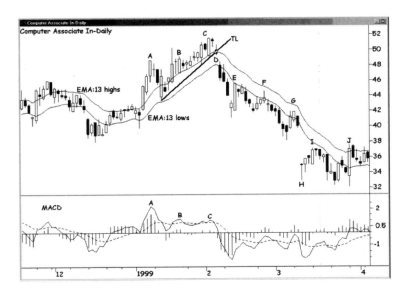

Figure 6.8 Computer Associates.

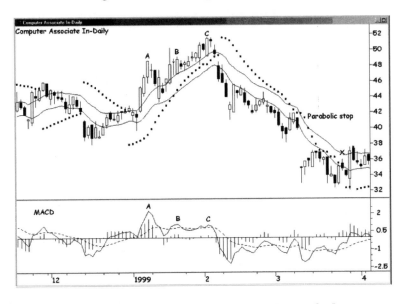

Figure 6.9 Computer Associates with parabolic stop.

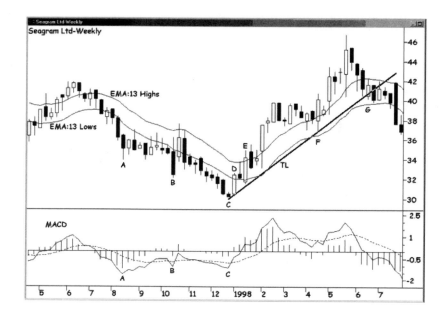

Figure 6.10   Seagram.

dles), and candle E is a bullish engulfing line. Buy on the candle after D when prices rise above the high of the morning star or at E when prices penetrate the top of the EMA channel. Trail a stop below the channel or below the bullish trendline connecting the swing lows at C and F. Exit on candle G when the trendline is broken or four weeks later (remember, it's a weekly chart) when prices fall below the bottom of the channel.

Figure 6.11 is a weekly chart of Intel (INTC). An interesting variation of a candlestick pattern begins two weeks before candle C with a tall, white candle. The next two candles have small real bodies that don't overlap the previous candle's real body. Candle D is a tall, black candle

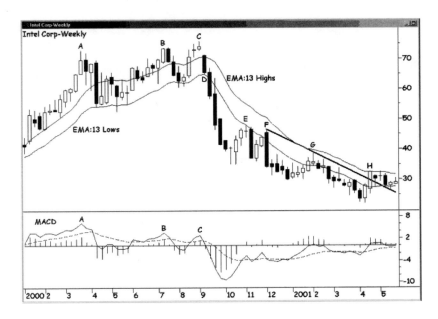

Figure 6.11   Intel.

that gaps away from candle C and closes well into the tall, white candle's real body, completing a very bearish evening star pattern. Also note the breakaway gap between candles C and D. Sell short on the candle after D below the low of D or below the low of the EMA channel. Trail a stop above the channel or at the swing highs (strength of two or greater) at E, F, and G. Exit on candle H above the trendline drawn from swing high F to swing high G, or exit above the channel.

Figure 6.12 is a 60-minute chart of Caterpillar (CAT). Candle D is a bullish engulfing line, so buy either on the candle after D, just above D's high, or three candles after D, when prices break through the top of the EMA

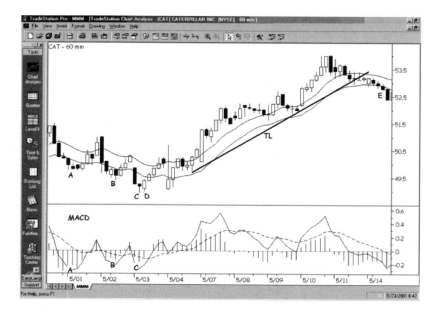

Figure 6.12 Caterpillar.

channel. Trail a stop below the channel and exit either on the trendline break six candles before E or on the decline below the channel three candles before E.

Figure 6.13 is a daily chart of British pound futures. Because the candle after C is a harami cross and the second candle of a tweezer top, it would be aggressive—but not unreasonable—to get a head start on this trade and buy on the second candle after C just above the tweezer top. Of course, the penetration of the top of the EMA channel one day later at D also provides a logical place to initiate a long position. Trail a stop just below the swing

150

Figure 6.13   British pound.

lows (strength of two or greater) at points E–I, and exit the trade on candle J.

Figure 6.14 is a very unusual daily chart of Canadian dollar futures. Instead of the more common three declines before the trend turns bullish, this downtrend posts five declines, and the MACD completes a complex, multiple divergence pattern from point A to point E. Note that prices did not penetrate the top of the EMA channel after swing lows C or D, so the strategy did not generate any false buy signals during this extended decline. Buy four days after E on the breakout above the

Figure 6.14 Canadian dollar.

channel and trail a stop just below the bullish trendline connecting swing lows F and G. Exit this trade at H, when the trendline is broken, or at I, when the channel is broken.

Figure 6.15 is a daily chart of Australian dollar futures. The candle after C is a harami, so selling short on the next candle just below the harami's low makes for a timely entry; alternatively, sell short on candle D when prices penetrate the bottom of the EMA channel. Trail a stop just above the swing highs (strength of two or greater) at E–I, and exit at J, when prices exceed the high of candle I.

Figure 6.15   Australian dollar.

Figure 6.16 is a daily chart of Dow futures. Candle D is a harami cross, so selling short on the next day just below the low of candle D is warranted; selling short on candle E when prices fall below the bottom of the EMA channel is also acceptable. Trail a stop above the channel or above swing highs F–I (strength of two or greater). There are two logical ways to exit this trade: (1) the three-candle pattern beginning with candle I is a morning star, so exit on candle J just above the previous candle's high, or (2) exit on candle K above the channel.

Figure 6.17 is a weekly chart of treasury notes. Note the tall upper shadow on candle D: The market probed

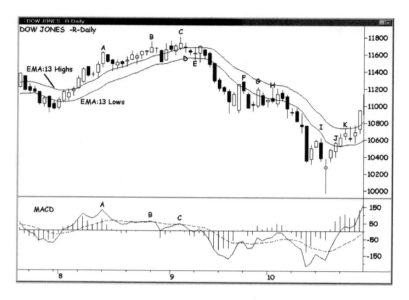

Figure 6.16   Dow futures.

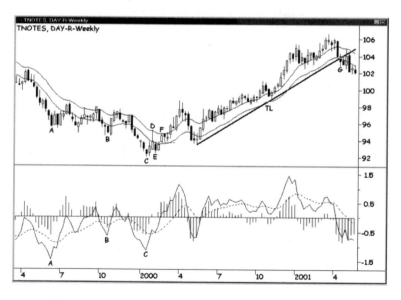

Figure 6.17   Treasury notes. (TL = trendline.)

154

the upside but failed to sustain its foray into higher ground. The black candle after candle D closed below the low of D, so it looked like the downtrend was back in force, despite the multiple bullish divergence pattern. In a situation like this—a failed test of the upside followed by a bearish candle—I like to buy if prices immediately make a second attempt to rally. In this example, I'd buy on candle F, when it gaps open above the tweezer top of the previous two candles. Trail a stop below the EMA channel and exit on candle G, which falls below the channel and below a bullish trendline.

Figure 6.18 is a weekly chart of soybean oil futures. Sell short on candle D, which penetrates the bottom of

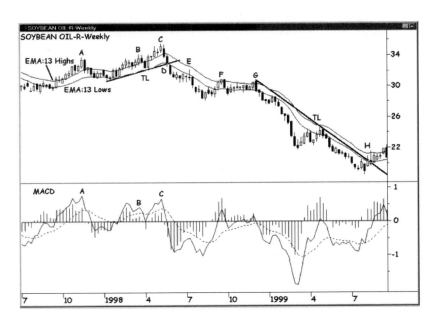

Figure 6.18   Soybean oil.

the EMA channel and breaks a bullish trendline. Trail a stop above swing highs F and G (strength of two or greater) and take profits on candle H when it breaks the bearish trendline.

Summary

Although the most ubiquitous piece of trading advice has always been to buy low and sell high, many authorities argue that it's impossible for traders to predict tops and bottoms. If they mean that traders rarely buy at the absolute low or sell at the absolute high of a major trend, they're right; if they mean that traders can't consistently buy *near* major bottoms or sell short *near* major tops, they're wrong. My *Triple Play* strategy buys soon after a market has completed three downward price swings and sells short soon after a market has completed three upward price swings. More importantly, *Triple Play* signals winning trades at these market turning points with enough accuracy and consistency to produce significant profits for traders who can follow the strategy with precision and steadfastness.

Chapter 6 Quiz

1. Changes in the price trend usually precede changes in the trend of momentum.

   True   False

2. In an uptrend, the MACD line's repeated failure to confirm new price highs suggests that a change in the trend may be imminent.

   True   False

   Note: The following questions refer specifically to the *Triple Play* strategy:

3. The setup is based on multiple divergence patterns between the MACD line and the signal line.

   True   False

4. The basic entry technique for a long position buys below the EMA channel.

   True   False

5. To improve on the strategy's basic entry technique, consider factors such as gaps, candlestick patterns, and trendlines.

   True   False

6. Candlestick patterns, trendlines, the EMA channel, the parabolic indicator, swing highs (if short), and swing lows (if long) can all be used to determine a trailing stop.

   True   False

Chapter 7

SUGGESTIONS FOR NEW TRADERS

It always fazes us a little to realize how many people spend so much time, money, and effort, apparently in a quest to discover the "hidden secrets" of the stock market. Mr. Average Man who has a few thousand dollars to invest and who may have a very keen understanding of his own business or profession, so often comes to Wall Street with the bright hope that he is going to find the magic word, or the crystal ball, or the unfailing oracle; a hope, by the way, that is not likely to be realized. It is not that he is unwilling to put forth further effort, or to spend money and time in his search. It is that he is searching in the wrong places for something that doesn't actually exist as he imagines it. No method, scheme, or plan that we know of can anticipate everything that may happen in the future. The most that one can hope to accomplish is to estimate the reasonably expectable consequences of a set of presently known conditions. There remains a big area of uncertainty; and an essential part of the investor's problem is to recognize this, accept it, and understand that a considerable part of his strategy must be to learn how to cope with conditions when they do not work out as he anticipated.

—John Magee, *Analyzing Bar Charts for Profit*
(John Magee Inc., Boston, 1994)

161

Here are five ideas that have helped me over the years as a trader. I hope you will find something useful in them as well.

1. When you are just starting out in trading, concentrate on learning technical analysis and improving your trading skills rather than focusing solely on the dollars won or lost. The money you win or lose while you are first learning to trade will not be of much consequence if you eventually become a successful trader. Trade only 100 shares of stock or one futures contract until you're sure you know what you're doing (and even then, increase your position size gradually).

2. If trading seems intimidating at first, remember that you will get used to it by following your trading strategy consistently over time. You will not always feel as uncomfortable as you do when you are making your first few trades. Imagine seeing for the first time a movie that is 10 times scarier than anything you've ever seen before. Now imagine seeing that same movie for the twentieth time: not so scary anymore, right? Same with trading.

3. Remember that the pain of missing out on a good trading opportunity that your strategy identified for you is much worse than losing on a trade that you entered and exited properly, according to your rules. When you're finding it difficult to "pull the trigger" and enter a new position, close your eyes, take some deep breaths, and visualize the chart

with prices moving strongly day after day in the right direction, but with you standing helplessly on the sidelines, kicking yourself and wishing you were a more disciplined trader. Then, visualize yourself entering the trade in accordance with your strategy's rules and getting stopped out the next day at your initial protective stop for a small loss. Which scenario hurts worse?

4. Do not expect certainty about a trade. You are looking for a preponderance of the evidence, not proof beyond a reasonable doubt. No trading setup is perfect: You can always find (or imagine) a reason why the trade might not work. Focus on *probabilities*—there are no sure things in trading.

5. Reaching your full potential as a trader is a lifelong process, not a get-rich-quick scheme. Don't let your trading successes and failures overwhelm other, more important, areas of your life, such as your family, friends, health, and happiness. At seminars I often say, "Trading is not a matter of life and death—it's much more important than that!" Of course, I'm joking. Although trading may become your *livelihood*, it should not become your *life*. Trade aggressively, trade with dedication and intensity, but don't forget to live wisely and well— then you'll really be playing for keeps!

Best wishes for (extremely) profitable trading,

Tom Bierovic

Appendix A

RECOMMENDED READING

When you enter the stock market, you are going into a competitive field in which your evaluations and opinions will be matched against some of the sharpest and toughest minds in business. You are in a highly specialized industry in which there are many different sectors, all of which are under intense study by men whose economic survival depends upon their best judgment. You will most certainly be exposed to advice, suggestions, offers of help from all sides. And, unless you are able to develop some market philosophy of your own, you will not be able to tell the good from the bad, the sound from the unsound.

—John Magee, Analyzing Bar Charts for Profit
(John Magee Inc., Boston, 1994)

167

Books About Trading and the Markets

Analyzing Bar Charts for Profit, John Magee, John Magee Inc., Boston, 1994

Candlestick Charting Explained, Gregory Morris, McGraw Hill, New York, 1995

Computer Analysis of the Futures Market, Charles LeBeau and David Lucas, Business One Irwin, Homewood, Illinois, 1992

Encyclopedia of Chart Patterns, Thomas Bulkowski, John Wiley & Sons, New York, 2000

Getting Started in Stocks, Alvin Hall, John Wiley & Sons, New York, 1996

How I Made $2,000,000 in the Stock Market, Nicolas Darvas, Kensington Publishing Corp., New York, 1986

Intermarket Technical Analysis, John Murphy, John Wiley & Sons, New York, 1991

Japanese Candlestick Charting Techniques, Steve Nison, New York Institute of Finance, New York, 1991

Market Wizards, Jack Schwager, New York Institute of Finance, New York, 1989

New Concepts in Technical Trading Systems, Trend Research, McLeansville, NC, 1978

The Disciplined Trader, Mark Douglas, New York Institute of Finance, New York, 1990

The Intuitive Trader, Robert Koppel, John Wiley & Sons, New York, 1996

The Nature of Risk: Stock Market Survival & the Meaning of Life, Justin Mamis, Addison-Wesley, New York, 1991

The New Market Wizards, Jack Schwager, John Wiley & Sons, New York, 1995

Real People; Real Traders, Adrienne Toghraie and Murray Ruggiero, Financial Times/Prentice Hall, New York, 2000

Reminiscences of a Stock Operator, Edward LeFevre, John Wiley & Sons, New York, 1994

Schwager on Futures: Technical Analysis, Jack Schwager, John Wiley & Sons, New York, 1994

Stock Market Wizards, Jack Schwager, HarperBusiness, New York, 2001

Technical Analysis and Stock Market Profits, Richard Schabacker, Pitman Publishing, London, 1997

Technical Analysis of Stock Trends, Eighth Edition, Robert Edwards and John Magee, AMACOM, New York, 2001

Technically Speaking, Chris Wilkinson, Traders Press, Greenville, South Carolina, 1997

Technical Analysis of the Financial Markets, John Murphy, New York Institute of Finance, New York, 1999

The Futures Game, Richard Tewles and Frank Bradley, McGraw-Hill, New York, 1998

The Psychology of Technical Analysis, Tony Plummer, Probus Publishing, Chicago, 1993

The Stock Market, Richard Tewles and Frank Bradley, John Wiley & Sons, New York, 1998

The Trading Rule That Can Make You Rich, Edward Dobson, Traders Press, Greenville, South Carolina, 1987

The Visual Investor, John Murphy, John Wiley & Sons, New York, 1996

Trade Your Way to Financial Freedom, Van Tharp, McGraw Hill, New York, 1998

Trading in the Zone, Mark Douglas and Thom Hartle, Prentice Hall, New York, 2001

Trading Systems and Methods, Third Edition, Perry Kaufman, John Wiley & Sons, New York, 1998

Trading With DiNapoli Levels, Joe DiNapoli, Coast Investment Software, Sarasota, Florida, 1997

Trading with Oscillators, Mark Etzkorn, John Wiley & Sons, New York, 1997

Traders Press, Inc. in Greenville, South Carolina, is a convenient and reliable source for these books and all other trading-related material. Their toll-free telephone number is (800) 927-8222, and their website is www.traderspress.com. Upon request, Traders Press will send you a free copy of their new 100-page catalog.

As a prelude to any technical study of the market, it would be well for the serious student to do some reading in psychology, perception, general semantics, etc., in order to understand the workings of his own mind, so that he can see clearly what he is trying to do and how he can apply new knowledge and experience.

—John Magee, *Analyzing Bar Charts for Profit*
(John Magee Inc., Boston, 1994)

Books About Thinking and Doing

A Brief History of Time, Stephen Hawking, Bantam Books, New York, 1998

A History of the Circle: Mathematical Reasoning and the Physical Universe, Ernest Zebrowski, Rutgers University Press, Piscataway, New Jersey, 1999

Against the Gods: The Remarkable Story of Risk, Peter Bernstein, John Wiley & Sons, New York, 1998

An Intelligent Person's Guide to Philosophy, Roger Scruton, Viking Penguin, New York, 1999

Aristotle For Everybody: Difficult Thought Made Easy, Mortimer Adler, Simon & Schuster, New York, 1997

Brunelleschi's Dome: How a Renaissance Genius Reinvented Architecture, Ross King, Penguin USA, 2001

Chaos: Making a New Science, James Gleick, Viking Penguin, New York, 1998

Copenhagen, a play, Michael Frayn, Vintage Anchor, New York, 1998

$E=mc^2$, *A Biography of the World's Most Famous Equation*, David Bodanis, Berkley Publishing Group, New York, 2001

Einstein's Dreams, Alan Lightman, Pantheon Books, New York, 1992

Fermat's Enigma: The Epic Quest to Solve the World's Greatest Mathematical Problem, Simon Singh, Walker & Co., New York, 1997

Flow: The Psychology of Optimal Experience, Mihaly Csikszentmihalyi, HarperCollins, New York, 1991

Longitude: The True Story of a Lone Genius Who Solved the Greatest Scientific Problem of His Time, Dava Sobel, Viking Penguin, New York, 1996

Seeing and Believing: How the Telescope Opened Our Eyes and Minds to the Heavens, Richard Panek, Penguin USA, 1999

Six Easy Pieces: Essentials of Physics Explained by Its Most Brilliant Teacher, Richard Feynman, Perseus Publishing, Cambridge, Massachusetts, 1996

NLP (neural-linguistic programming): The New Technology of Achievement, Steve Andreas and Charles Faulkner, Morrow William, New York, 1996

The Crowd & Extraordinary Popular Delusions, Gustave Le Bon and Charles MacKay, Traders Press, Greenville, South Carolina, 1996

The Lessons of History, Will and Ariel Durant, Simon & Schuster, New York, 1968

The Nothing That Is: A Natural History of Zero, Robert Kaplan, Oxford University Press, New York, 2000

The Story of Philosophy, Will Durant, Simon & Schuster, New York, 1976

Walden, Henry David Thoreau, Washington Square Press, New York, 1968

Zen in the Art of Archery, Eugen Herrigel, Random House, New York, 1999

Recommended Publications

Active Trader magazine
www.activetradermag.com.

Formula Research: Quantitative Treatment of the Financial Markets
Nelson F. Freeburg, editor
800.720.1080 or 901.756.8607

Moore Research Center, Inc.
Seasonal analysis of the futures markets
www.mrci.com
800.927.7259

Technical Analysis of Stocks and Commodities magazine
www.traders.com

Appendix B

ANSWERS TO
CHAPTER QUIZZES

Chapter 1

1. False. The startup costs and overhead expenses for trading are much *lower* than for most other businesses.
2. False. Most traders would be more successful (and less stressed out) if they did *not* watch the markets tick by tick throughout the trading day.
3. True.
4. False. Only about *10%* of traders are consistent winners, but they are extremely well rewarded for their skill and effort. It is difficult—but not prohibitively so—to make it into the top 10%.

Chapter 2

1. False. Stock prices usually fluctuate in extremely varied price swings. Their duration and magnitude are hard to predict.
2. True.
3. False. By definition, critical points in the markets are tricky situations. A simple "one-size-fits-all" solution is not available.
4. True.

Chapter 3

1. False. An *entry* technique is only one piece of the puzzle. Successful trading also requires setups, exits, money management, and self-discipline.
2. True.
3. False. When a trader identifies a setup, he should turn his attention to his *entry* technique. The setup conditions and entry conditions are separate components of a good trading strategy. *Buying as soon as possible* is usually not the best entry condition; in fact, it's not really an entry condition at all.
4. True.
5. False. A trailing stop is set *below* the current price in a long position and *above* the current price in a short position.
6. True.
7. True.

Chapter 4

1. True.
2. False. Impulse waves are usually *longer* in duration and *larger* in magnitude than corrective waves.
3. False. The *first* corrective wave of a trend is the most likely to provide a good entry. Corrections

after the first one are not as reliable (my *R2D2* reverse-divergence setup is an exception).

4. True.

5. False. On a daily candlestick chart, a white (or hollow) real body means that today's close was *above today's open;* a black (or filled) real body means that today's close was *below today's open.*

6. True.

7. True.

8. False. *Support* is like a floor; *resistance* is like a ceiling.

9. False. The swing low would have a strength of *three.*

10. True.

11. False. If today's low is above yesterday's close, today's true range is today's high minus yesterday's *close.*

12. False. A new 21-day low usually indicates a bearish *impulse* wave.

13. True.

14. True.

15. True.

16. False. The MACD histogram is the difference between the *MACD line* and the signal line.

17. False. When the MACD *line*—not the MACD *histogram*—crosses above zero, it means that the fast EMA has crossed above the slow EMA.

18. True.

19. False. A DMI spread above zero only tells us that the trend is up; it doesn't tell us that the trend is *strong*. When the DMI spread reaches +15 or higher, we know that the stock is in a *strong* uptrend.

20. False. The parabolic dots rise *every* day in an uptrend, not only on days that make new highs for the trade. (The only exception is a case in which the dot would be placed inside the previous day's range; in that case, the dot would not be moved.)

21. True.

22. True.

23. False. *First Prize* buys after a decline in an uptrend and sells short after a rally in a downtrend.

24. True.

25. True.

26. False. In a buy setup, the DMI spread has to reach +15 or higher at the high of the impulse wave. It usually *won't* remain above +15 during the corrective wave.

27. False. The close has to be at least a 38.2% retracement, but not more than a 61.8% retracement. In other words, the close has to be *between* those levels; it doesn't have to settle *at* one of those levels.

28. True.

29. False. The MACD histogram must be falling (i.e., it must be lower than it was yesterday) before an order to sell short can be placed.

30. False. Place the buy order above the previous day's high.

31. True.

32. False. The strategy works well on both stocks and futures, and it can be applied to various time frames, from intraday to weekly.

Chapter 5

1. True.

2. True.

3. False. Normal divergences occur in the *opposite* direction of the trend. A bullish divergence, for example, may appear after a stock makes a low, rallies, and then falls to a lower low.

4. True.

5. False. For a bearish setup, the MACD line must form a *reverse-divergence* low. In *Playing for Keeps*, we don't trade single occurrences of normal divergences: We trade reverse divergences and multiple normal divergences (see the *Triple Play* strategy).

6. True.

7. True.

Chapter 6

1. False. Changes in the trend of *momentum* usually precede changes in the *price* trend.
2. True.
3. False. The setup is based on multiple divergences between the MACD line and price lows.
4. False. The basic entry technique for a long position buys *above* the EMA channel.
5. True.
6. True.

GLOSSARY

average true range   True range is the largest of the following: today's high minus today's low, today's high minus yesterday's close, or yesterday's close minus today's low. Average true range is a moving average of true range. Welles Wilder introduced this indicator in his 1978 classic, *New Concepts in Technical Trading Systems*.

bar chart   A daily bar chart represents a market's daily trading activity. The high-low range is drawn as a vertical line, and the open and close are drawn as tick marks to the vertical bar's left and right, respectively. Bar charts can be based on any time period; for example, a bar chart could show the trading activity for one minute, one day, or one month.

corrective wave   A corrective wave is a price swing against the direction of the trend. Corrective waves are usually shorter in duration and smaller in magnitude than impulse waves.

critical point A critical point in an uptrend is a price decline from above a moving-average channel into the channel. A critical point in a downtrend is a price rally from below a moving-average channel into the channel. At critical points, traders must decide if the countertrend price move is a short-term reaction within the existing trend or the beginning of a trend reversal.

directional movement index Directional movement is the largest part of today's range that is outside yesterday's range. The directional movement index is composed of three lines that together indicate whether a stock or commodity is in a trending mode or a trading range. The DMI spread is the difference between the positive and negative directional movement lines. This indicator was introduced in 1978 by Welles Wilder in *New Concepts in Technical Trading Systems*.

divergence Divergence is a condition that occurs when a technical indicator does not confirm a new price high or low. A bearish-divergence top indicates that bullish momentum was weaker at the current high than it was at the previous (lower) high; a bullish-divergence bottom means that bearish momentum was weaker on the current low than on the previous (higher) low.

entries An entry is the component of a trading strategy that triggers a new long or short position while the setup component is in effect.

exits   An exit is the component of a trading strategy that closes out a position. Common types of exits include initial protective stops, breakeven stops, trailing stops, and profit targets.

exponential moving average   Like simple moving averages, exponential moving averages (EMAs) smooth price data to make the trend easier to discern. Unlike simple moving averages, however, EMAs give more weight to recent data and don't abruptly drop old data when it falls outside the moving average's time window. An EMA channel is composed of an EMA of highs and an EMA of lows instead of the more common EMA of closes.

Fibonacci retracement zone   A Fibonacci retracement zone extends from a 38.2% correction of an impulse wave to a 61.8% correction. A market's pullback into the retracement zone frequently offers a low-risk/high-reward trading opportunity.

First Prize   *First Prize* is a trading strategy that buys after the first decline in a strong uptrend and sells short after the first rally in a strong downtrend.

impulse wave   An impulse wave is a price swing in the direction of the trend. Impulse waves are usually longer in duration and larger in magnitude than their counterpart, corrective waves.

initial protective stop   An initial protective stop limits the risk on a trade by automatically exiting a position when prices move in a counter-to-anticipated direction. Initial protective stops can be based on chart points, average true range, a fixed dollar amount, or other criteria.

Japanese candlestick charts   A Japanese candlestick chart is a visual representation of a market's price activity. A candle's real body represents a day's open and close, and its upper and lower shadows represent the day's high and low. Over the centuries, the Japanese have discovered many candlestick patterns that can help the chartist to forecast the continuation or reversal of a trend. Steve Nison introduced Japanese candlestick charts to the Western world in 1991 in his book, *Japanese Candlestick Charting Techniques*.

MACD   The moving average convergence-divergence (MACD) was developed by Gerald Appel in the 1970s. It consists of three components: the MACD line, the signal line, and the MACD histogram. The MACD line is the difference between a fast and a slow exponential moving average (EMA). The signal line is an EMA of the MACD line. The MACD histogram is the difference between the MACD line and the signal line. A unique characteristic of the MACD indicator is that it has the ability to measure a market's momentum (the acceleration or deceleration of its price changes) without losing its ability to also follow a trend.

momentum oscillator   A momentum oscillator is any technical indicator that measures the acceleration or deceleration of a market's price changes. Examples include the momentum and rate-of-change

186

indicators, the MACD, the relative strength index (RSI), and stochastics.

parabolic indicator   The parabolic indicator plots a series of rising dots in an uptrend and a series of falling dots in a downtrend. In a new uptrend, the series of dots begins at the low of the previous downtrend; in a new downtrend, the series of dots begins at the high of the previous uptrend. As a market makes new highs in an uptrend or new lows in a downtrend, the parabolic's dots accelerate their movement to lock in increasing amounts of profits. The parabolic indicator was introduced by Welles Wilder in 1978 in *New Concepts in Technical Trading Systems*.

price channel   A price channel consists of the highest high and lowest low of a specified number of days. Breakouts to new *n*-day highs and lows often portend significant price trends in the direction of the breakout.

price swing   In *Playing for Keeps*, a bullish price swing extends from the lowest close below a moving-average channel to the highest close above the channel. A bearish price swing extends from the highest close above a moving-average channel to the lowest close below the channel.

profit target   A profit target is used to exit a trade at a specified objective—for example, at $45 for a stock purchased at $35.

R2D2   The *R2D2* strategy is based on a reverse-divergence pattern between the MACD line and prices. Reverse divergences, which occur in the direction of the trend they're measuring, are usually more reliable than normal divergences, which occur against the direction of the trend.

resistance   Resistance is a price level at which sellers are strong enough to overpower buyers. Resistance is like a ceiling above a market's current price.

reverse divergence   Reverse divergence is a technical pattern formed by prices and a momentum oscillator. In the bullish case, prices hold above their previous low while the oscillator falls to a lower low; in the bearish case, prices hold below their previous high while the oscillator rises to a higher high.

setups   Setups are the technical conditions that tell us that market conditions may be favorable for a winning trade. With a setup in place, a trader turns his attention to his entry technique. Most trading strategies perform better with separate setup and entry conditions.

simple moving average   A simple moving average smooths price data to make the trend easier to discern. To calculate a 21-day simple moving average of closes, for example, add the last 21 closes and divide the total by 21.

strategies   Trading strategies are the rules that specify a trader's setup, entry, and exit conditions. Strategies also often include rules about market selection, money management, and portfolio management.

support   Support is a price level at which buyers are
strong enough to overpower sellers. Support is like a
floor below a market's current price.

swing high   A swing high is a price high with a
specified minimum number of lower highs to its
immediate left and right. Swing highs often act as
resistance above a market's current price.

swing low   A swing low is a price low with a specified
minimum number of higher lows to its immediate
left and right. Swing lows often act as support below
a market's current price.

trailing stop   Trailing stops, which are set below
current prices in a long position and above current
prices in a short position, attempt to lock in some
profits while giving a market some room to run.
Trailing stops are usually adjusted higher in a long
trade as prices rise and are adjusted lower in a short
trade as prices fall.

Triple Play   The *Triple Play* strategy is based on
multiple normal divergences between the MACD line
and prices. As might be expected, multiple
divergences generally provide more accurate trade
setups than single divergences.

INDEX

191